Lost Cities of Asia

Ceylon Pagan Angkor

Lost Cities of Asia

by Wim Swaan

G.P. Putnam's Sons New York

First American Edition 1966

Library of Congress Catalog Card
Number : 66-25448

Designed by Harold Bartram

Printed in Italy by
ISTITUTO ITALIANO D'ARTI GRAFICHE
BERGAMO

Contents

Acknowledgements

I should like to express a special debt of gratitude to Professor G. H. Luce of Rangoon University, authority on the ancient culture of Pagan, for filling in several details of the historical background, providing an annotated map for my visit and sketching out my itinerary. Without his help I should have missed much of interest. My sincere thanks are due to the Archaeological Survey of Burma for arranging accommodation in the Circuit House at Pagan and furnishing a most able guide and transport; to the authorities in both Ceylon and Cambodia for their kind cooperation, and to the National Museum at Phnom Penh, the Musée Guimet, the British Museum and the Boston Museum of Fine Arts for permission to photograph works of art in their collections. The Trustees of the British Museum have kindly given their permission to reproduce text figures 2, 3, 5, 9, 10 and 11.

W.S.

List of Plates

Illustrations in text

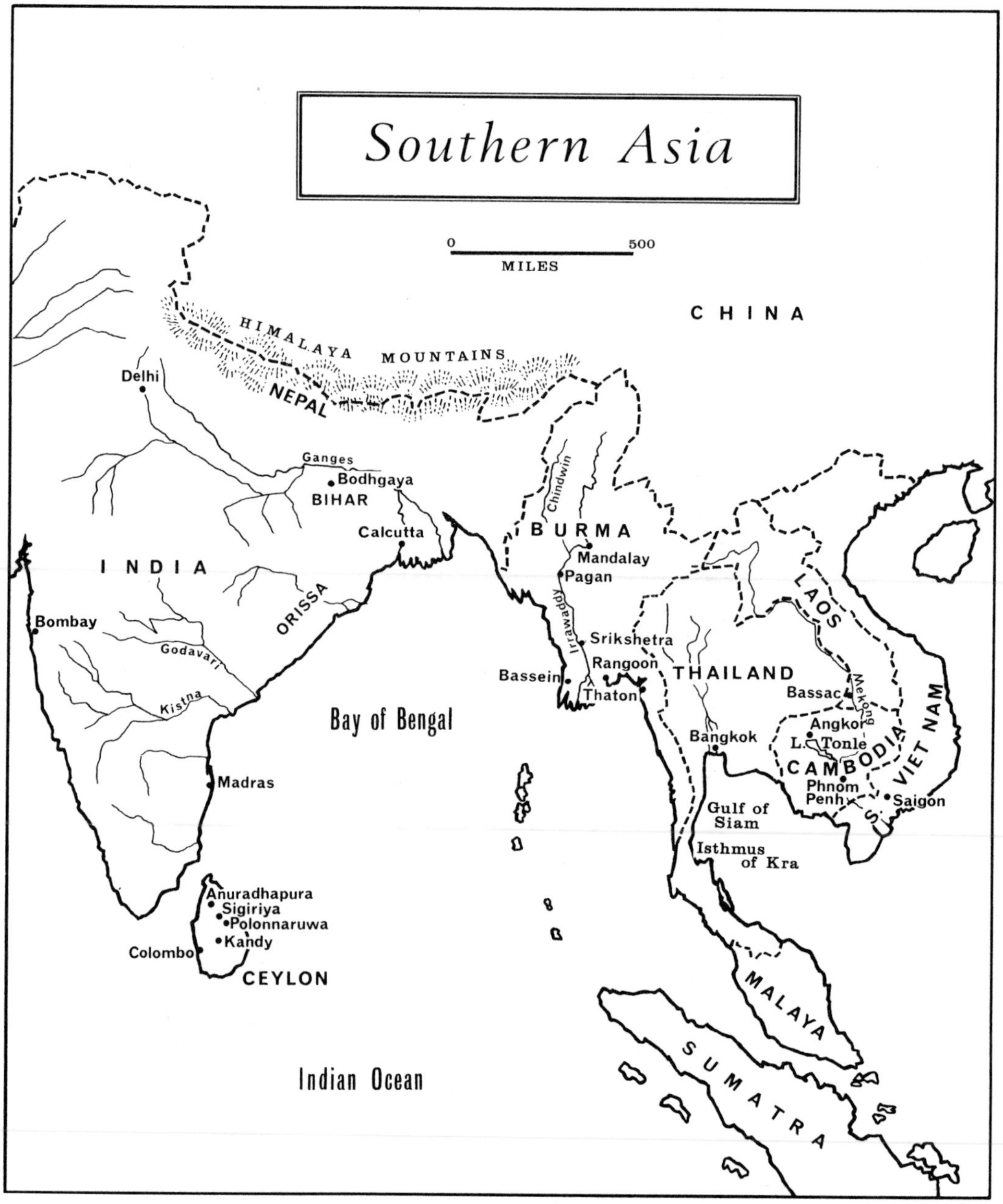

Southern Asia
0
500
MILES
CHINA
HIMALAYA MOUNTAINS
NEPAL
Delhi
Ganges
Bodhgaya
BIHAR
Calcutta
INDIA
ORISSA
Bombay
Godavari
Kistna
Madras
Bay of Bengal
Anuradhapura
Sigiriya
Polonnaruwa
Kandy
Colombo
CEYLON
Indian Ocean
Chindwin
BURMA
Mandalay
Pagan
Irrawaddy
Srikshetra
Rangoon
Bassein
Thaton
THAILAND
LAOS
Mekong
Bassac
Angkor
L. Tonle
CAMBODIA
Phnom Penh
S. VIET NAM
Saigon
Bangkok
Gulf of Siam
Isthmus of Kra
MALAYA
SUMATRA

Introduction

The Heritage of India

On the site of the ancient city of Polonnaruwa in Ceylon a solitary herdsman tending his water-buffalo disturbs the vigil of the disciple Ananda, mourning over the gigantic, rock-cut image of the Buddha passing into *nirvana*; fishermen on the broad reaches of the Irrawaddy River at Pagan in Burma haul in their nets against the backdrop of a thousand pagodas mouldering in picturesque decay; in the twilight gloom of the Cambodian jungle a snake slithers over the sensuous limbs of a celestial maiden, petrified in a seductive pose of her dance in honour of a God-king of lost Angkor.

These relics of past grandeur – so reminiscent in their pastoral setting of Piranesi engravings of classical ruins – bear mute testimony to one of the least-known yet most glorious chapters in the history of mankind: that of the classical cultures of 'Greater India'.

It was India, at the apogee of her glory and ranking with China and Rome as the three great centres of world culture during the first centuries of our era, that brought the flame of civilization to all three areas and imposed the indelible stamp of her religious, philosophical, technical and artistic heritage.

Between India and Rome there was a flourishing trade. By the beginning of our era some hundred and twenty Roman ships alone are estimated to have been engaged annually in the India trade. Westwards went gems and fine textiles, perfumes, drugs and spices, cane sugar and ivory, elephants, tigers and buffaloes for the circuses, and tame monkeys, parrots and peacocks for the patrician ladies of Rome. Indian iron and steel, famed for its strength and purity, was exported from a very early date. There is a record of a gift of 100 talents of steel (*ferrum candidum*) to Alexander the Great by the rulers of the Punjab.

To the China market went frankincense and myrrh, fine carpets and Middle-Eastern textiles, pottery and glassware.

India herself seems to have wanted little that the west could offer – except gold. The balance of trade was so unfavourable to Rome, that legislation had later to be introduced to curb the eastward drain on her gold reserves.

Roman ships seem never to have penetrated much further than Ceylon and the East coast of India, but Indian merchants plied their trade as far as the ports of South China in vessels capable of carrying as much as a thousand tons of cargo and seven hundred passengers, making possible trade and also migration, on an exceptionally large scale.

This adventurous voyaging far abroad was given great impetus by the triumph of a new Indian religion, which removed the danger of ritual contamination by contact with strangers – a very real risk to the caste- and race-conscious devotees of Brahmanism.

By the middle of the first millennium B.C. two constant and fundamental concepts of Indian religious thought had already been firmly established: firstly, that every thought and action sets in motion an inexorable chain of cause and effect; secondly, a belief in the transmigration of souls, death merely constituting a passage between innumerable existences. Actions might bear their inevitable fruit either in this life or in a future existence, the form taken in the reincarnation – divine, human, animal or demonic – being determined by the merit or demerit acquired in previous existences (*karma*).

The socio-political 'caste' system which enabled the Indo-Aryan conquerors to maintain their hegemony despite their numerical inferiority was perfectly integrated with this religious concept in what might be termed a divinely-appointed system of *apartheid*. Inferior caste – the result of misdeeds in previous existences – could only be transcended in the next incarnation by good conduct in this life, including acceptance of one's caste and of the constraints it imposed. Revolt was not only an anti-social but an irreligious act. The Sacred Books also maintained the identity of the 'Innermost Self' with the 'Absolute', or the 'Universal Being' (*Brahman*). To arrive at a cognition of this truth through ascetic practices or magical ritual was to achieve release from the endless cycle of birth and rebirth.

To these concepts were added, towards the end of the sixth century B.C., the teachings of the Buddha. Siddartha Gautama was a prince of the Sakya Clan ruling over a region near the border of present-day Nepal. His conception and birth were accompanied by many miracles and a prophesy that he would become a great leader, either temporal or spiritual. His ambitious father was determined that it should be the former and to this end had his son confined within the palace walls and kept from all things unpleasant, lest they encourage an introspective frame of mind. One day the young prince escaped from the palace and had a symbolic encounter with the harsh realities of life in the form of a beggar (poverty), a sick man (illness) and a corpse (death). Disillusioned by the inevitability of sorrow, he renounced his life of princely luxury and ease, and left his wife and infant son to become a mendicant ascetic. Through years of study under celebrated ascetics, and by penance and self-mortification, he endeavoured to unravel the secret of existence, but it continually eluded him until one day, seated in meditation beneath a Bo-tree at Bodhgaya, the 'Eternal Truth' came to him and he became the Buddha or 'Enlightened One'.

The kernel of Buddhist philosophy is contained in 'The Sermon of the Turning of the Wheel of the Law' preached in the Deer Park at Benares, which occupies a similar position in Buddhism to The Sermon on the Mount. Its basic tenets may be summarized as follows: sorrow is inherent in life and stems from the craving of the Ego. It can only be overcome by detachment from desire, and this is best achieved through 'The Middle Way' of the 'Noble Eightfold Path' of Right Views, Right Resolve, Right Speech, Right Conduct, Right Livelihood, Right Effort, Right Recollection and Right Meditation (1). This path of progressive detachment leads ultimately to an extinction of Self, an escape from the cycle of birth and rebirth with its attendant suffering, and *nirvana*, a blissful state of Non-Existence or reabsorption into the Absolute.

The marked similarity between *nirvana* in its optimistic interpretation and the principle of *Brahman* is hardly surprising, for Buddhism could in many respects be considered a reform movement within Brahmanism. Socially, however, its tenets were no less than revolutionary, for Buddhism rejected the entire caste system and addressed to all men its twin message of detachment from desire and compassion towards fellow beings with whom one is united by a common bond of suffering.

Initially, but one of a number of reformed sects – for example its contemporary, Jainism – Buddhism started on its career as a world religion with the conversion in the third century B.C. of the Emperor Asoka of the Mauryan Dynasty. This humane and able ruler, the perfect exemplar of Plato's 'philosopher-king', was an ardent proselytizer of his new-found faith and sent missionaries throughout his Empire and far beyond to spread the creed of the Buddha.

There are two main schools of Buddhist thought. The earlier Hinayana Doctrine is primarily philosophical, and is dedicated to the ideal of individual salvation, preferably through monastic discipline, and without any possibility of supernatural aid. This was the message carried by Asoka's missionaries and which, in essence, survives as the religion of both Ceylon and South-East Asia today. The name Hinayana (literally: the little or lesser boat or vehicle) was given this orthodox form to distinguish it from a later development, the Mahayana, which arose in the first or second century A.D. Idealistic and mystical, and with complex metaphysical connotations, it propounded the ideal of salvation for all, hence Mahayana, the 'great boat or vehicle', in which all mankind can ride (2).

Mahayana Buddhism saw the final transformation of Prince Gautama from a spiritual super-man into a god. According to its doctrine, the historic Buddha was, however, but one in a long line of Buddhas or 'Enlightened Ones', past and future. It posited the possibility of the transfer of merit from Bodhisattvas, saintly beings who have earned their Buddhahood but have elected to forego the bliss of *nirvana* yet a short while in order to help others to attain salvation. Through their mediation it was possible to circumvent the inexorable 'Law of Cause and Effect', and attain sooner to *nirvana*, which was now no longer limited to the concept of 'Blissful Extinction', but tended to approach a celestial paradise.

Concurrent with the rise of the Mahayana Doctrine, India saw a reassertion of the power of Brahmanism, but a Brahmanism so infused with the philosophy and humanitarian spirit of Buddhism as to constitute a new religion: Hinduism. Brahmanism had, in fact, answered the challenge of its rival in a manner typical of the East: not with open force, but by appropriating many of its most appealing features. The older gods of Brahmanism gradually took a subordinate place and were superseded by three deities: Brahma, the Creator; Vishnu, the Preserver; and Siva, the Destroyer; together constituting the *Trimurti* or Triad, which in turn was but a manifestation of the *Brahman* or Universal Being. With its pantheon of myriads of deities presided over by the *Trimurti*, Hinduism thus embraced a variety of religious expression ranging from primitive idol worship to abstract speculation of a monotheistic nature.

Brahma, the Creator (not to be confused with the *Brahman* or Universal Being) was soon completely overshadowed by Vishnu and Siva. Since death opens up the way for new life, Siva gradually came to be regarded as the God of both Destruction and Creation, the latter attribute symbolized by his worship in the form of a *lingam* or phallus. It was this benevolent, creative aspect of the god which was to be dominant in the Sivaite Cults of South-East Asia.

Both Buddhism and Hinduism incorporated and sublimated many primitive animistic and fertility cults. To assume particular importance was the worship of the *naga* or serpent-deity, regarded both as the guardian of treasure locked in the earth and as the beneficent spirit of the waters. Embodied in the form of a regal, multi-headed, hooded cobra, the *naga* would become the very *leitmotiv* of the art of Angkor.

The Gupta Period (320-550 A.D.) constituted the Golden Age of Indian culture. Hinduism in a particularly tolerant and creative phase was already dominant, but Buddhism continued to flourish with the Mahayana variant gaining strength. The administration was a model of efficiency, justice and clemency. Hospitals and charitable institutions provided free care for the sick and poor – even from other countries. Trade flourished. Visitors from abroad all commented on the prosperity of the country, the high standard of living and the unusual degree of personal freedom. Travellers could proceed throughout the realm in complete safety and without passports or special permission. Literature, the drama, the dance and the plastic arts all flourished under enlightened court patronage and received their classic expression. Gupta India in its heyday could well claim to be the best-governed and most civilized country in the world.

Such was the culture and the extraordinarily rich and complex body of religion and philosophy which Indian traders and missionaries carried throughout 'Greater India'. To these lands she brought also her knowledge in irrigation, husbandry and metallurgy, mathematics and astronomy, a literary language and an alphabet (3).

Significantly, the cultural dominance of India was achieved not through force, but by the voluntary acceptance of her manifestly superior gifts on the part of eager and apt pupils. This was in marked contrast to the southward march of China, an armed expansion on the regular Roman model.

A fascinating question, and one which has had a far-reaching effect on world history, is why China – particularly in the case of Indo-China – did not exercise a dominant influence during these early years. Several factors contributed. China's traditional major link with India and the civilizations of the Middle East was the overland 'Silk Route' across Central Asia. Though geographically so much nearer than India, she initially evinced comparatively little interest in her 'southern barbarian' neighbours and the officials at China's southern ports, if anything, discouraged private trading ventures with the south. Chinese ships and navigation methods were both greatly inferior. Long after Indian, Malay and Arab ships were able to strike out boldly across the open seas, Chinese ships were still forced to hug the shore, and this made them all the more vulnerable to the attacks of the numerous pirates that infested the waters off her southernmost provinces, which the authorities did so little to suppress, perhaps precisely because of meagre official interest in the area. Finally, it must be borne in mind, that the zenith of Indian power during the Gupta Period coincided with a most unsettled period in Chinese history. With the reunification of China under the T'ang Dynasty in the seventh century A.D., there was a vastly increased Chinese interest in the lands to the south.

Thanks to its geographical situation, Ceylon remained within the Indian sphere of influence; South-East Asia, for the same reason, was destined ultimately to fall within the Chinese orbit – but only after the impressionable formative years, when her culture had already been set in an Indian mould and when Chinese culture itself had been much influenced by Buddhist (Indian) thought. Indeed, the whole of Asia was to remain forever heavily in debt to India. As Ananda Coomaraswamy so aptly put it 'although Far-Eastern races developed independently elements of culture no less important than those of India – almost all that belongs to the common spiritual consciousness of Asia, the ambient in which its diversities are reconcilable, is of Indian origin' (4).

In each country to which she brought her culture the initial period of 'Indianization' which tended merely to mirror the parent culture, gradually evolved in a distinctive manner and finally burst into a spectacular flowering of the national genius amply attested to by the noble ruins of Anuradhapura, Sigiriya and Polonnaruwa in Ceylon, Pagan in Burma and Angkor in Cambodia that are the subject of this book.

1 Bronze votive statuette of a female divinity found at Polonnaruwa, Ceylon. *British Museum, London*

2 'Naga' or Serpent Divinity; decorative stele, Anuradhapura, Ceylon

3 Dwarf 'Dvarapala' or 'Gateway Guardian', Anuradhapura, Ceylon

4 Sacred pool and rock-cut temple of Isurumuniya, Anuradhapura, Ceylon

2

3

5

6

7

8

9

1 Ceylon

Anuradhapura

The Sacred City of the Bo-Tree

The isle of Ceylon depends like a drop-pearl from the southern tip of the sub-continent of India. Its shape has been compared to a pear, a pearl, a mango fruit, even by the Dutch conquerors to a Westphalian ham. All the analogies, poetic or prosaic, are suggestive of wealth and abundance. So, too, the names by which the island has been known from earliest times. To the Chinese and the Tamils of South-India alike, it was 'The Isle of Gems', to the merchants of Arabia 'The Isle of Delight', while to the Sinhalese themselves it has always been *Sri Lanka*, 'The Resplendent Isle'. Lanka, too, is the name used in the Ramayana, greatest of the trilogy of epic poems on which Indian history is based. This relates the abduction of Sita, bride of Rama by Ravana, the demon-king of Ceylon; the invasion of Lanka with the aid of an army of monkeys under the command of the monkey-general, Hanuman, who built a bridge of boulders across the narrow straits separating the island from the mainland; and the rescue of Sita. To the sceptical Western mind at most a fascinating allegory of an early Aryan raid on Lanka – complete with justifiable provocation – it should be remembered that to the hundreds of millions of Hindus this tale is invested with the same authority as the events of the Old Testament, and that Hanuman, the monkey-god, is still worshipped throughout India.

The gems and spices of Ceylon and its convenient location as an *entrepot*, brought merchants early to its shores. Fa-Hsien, the Chinese pilgrim-traveller, relates that 'the island originally had no human inhabitants, but was occupied by dryads and *nagas* (serpent deities) with whom the merchants of various countries carried on a trade. When the trafficking was taking place, the spirits did not show themselves. They simply set forth their precious commodities, with labels of the price attached to them, while the merchants made their purchases according to the price, and took the things away.' (5)

The earliest European account of Ceylon, twenty years after the death of Alexander the Great, came from Megasthenes, a Seleucid envoy to India, who spoke from hearsay of its elephants, gold and jewels. Pliny (6) personally interviewed the Sinhalese envoys to Rome during the reign of the Emperor Claudius, and Ptolemy included a description of Ceylon in his monumental *Geographia* with the capital, Anuradhapura, *Anurogrammum Regium.*

The scholar dealing with the ancient cultures of Ceylon has the great advantage of a unique body of historical literature: the *Mahavamsa* or Chronicle of the 'Greater Dynasty', and the later *Culavamsa* or 'Lesser Dynasty'. (7) Together, these trace in one continuous narrative, the history of the Sinhalese from their arrival in Ceylon in the fifth century B.C. up to the deposition of the last king of Kandy by the British in 1815. The authors of both chronicles were *bhikkhus* or Buddhist monks and their religious bias must be taken into account in assessing the material. Although recorded in a highly poetic style, liberally embroidered with miracle and invention, the chronicles are, in essence, surprisingly accurate.

5 Life-size, gilded-bronze image of Pattini Devi from Ceylon. *British Museum, London*

6 The Thuparama Dagoba enshrining the collar-bone (relic) of the Buddha, Anuradhapura, Ceylon

7 'The Lovers'; bas-relief at Isurumuniya, Anuradhapura, Ceylon

8 The Ruanweli Dagoba, Anuradhapura, Ceylon

9 The Tissawewa 'Tank' and distant Ruanweli Dagoba, Anuradhapura, Ceylon

The *Mahavamsa* relates the legend of the founding of the Sinhalese race. The king of the Vanga people in India had a daughter 'very fair and very amorous' of whom it was foretold that she would mate with the king of the beasts. 'For shame the king and the queen could not suffer her' and the princess, 'desiring the joy of an independent life', disguised herself and joined a caravan travelling to another country. En route they were attacked by a lion, and all her companions fled. The princess, however, mindful of the prophecy, went to meet the lion. The lion was smitten with love and came towards her 'with wagging tail and ears laid back'. The princess fearlessly caressed him, arousing the lion to fiercest passion by her touch, and he carried her off to his cave as his mate. Twins, a boy and a girl, were born of this strange union. The son, whose hands were formed like the paws of a lion, was named Sinhabahu, or 'Lion-arm'. When he was sixteen years old, he questioned his mother on the doubt that had long troubled him 'Wherefore are you and our father so different, dear Mother?' When she had told him all, he suggested they return to the world of men, and one day when the father was away in search of prey, Sinhabahu rolled away the great stone at the entrance to the cave, took his mother on his right shoulder and his young sister on his left, and fled. The three eventually reached a border village, under the command of a son of the princess's uncle and after various miraculous events the nymphomaniac princess married her cousin and together they all returned to the Vanga capital.

The lion, grieving over his lost family, would neither eat nor drink and ravaged the border-villages in search of them. In desperation the king offered an ever larger reward to anyone who could rid his kingdom of the enraged animal. Twice Sinhabahu was dissuaded by his mother from accepting the challenge, but when the reward was increased for the third time, he could resist the temptation no longer. He returned to his home and when the lion saw him at the mouth of the cave 'he came forward for love of his son', who heartlessly shot him. The arrow struck the lion's forehead but because of the lion's tenderness towards his son, it rebounded and fell on the earth at the youth's feet. And so it fell out three times, until the king of the beasts grew wrathful and the arrow pierced his body. After this despicable act, which will most certainly have alienated all animal lovers, Sinhabahu returned in triumph to the capital with the head and mane of his father. The old king had just died without an heir and the ministers requested Sinhabahu to be their ruler. He accepted the honour, but delegated his authority to his mother's new husband and left for the land of his birth with his sister. There he built a city and reigned with his sister as his queen. She bore him twin sons sixteen times.

When the eldest son, Vijayo ('Victory'), grew to manhood, he was appointed prince-regent by his father, but 'committed many intolerable deeds of violence'. In vain the king attempted to reform his son and heir until, eventually, he could no longer disregard the voice of his outraged people demanding the death of Vijayo. 'And he caused Vijayo and seven hundred of his unruly followers to be shaven over half the head' – the traditional mark of a slave – put them on a ship and sent them forth. After a long voyage they reached the shores of Lanka and fell exhausted on the beach, staining their palms in the red-laterite soil and thus giving the island the name by which it was to be known in the West for centuries: Taprobane, from *Tambapanni* or 'Copper-hand'. (8)

This historic arrival of the founding-father was placed by the chronicles on the very day 'that the Tathagata (Buddha) lay down between the two *Sala*-trees and passed into *nirvana*'. (9)

The subsequent encounter of Vijayo and his companions with a *Yakkhini* princess and sorceress named Kuveni bears such a striking resemblance to the Ulysses-Circe legend as to have led some scholars to look for a common origin.

After outwitting the sorceress with divine aid – for as with Aeneas, the importance of his mission assured the founding-father the personal protection of the gods – Vijayo won her over to his side and married Kuveni. But although she was so far loyal to her new husband as to betray her own people to be massacred by the newcomers and bore Vijayo two children, he tired of her and refused to be consecrated king before he had a queen of noble birth. And so for reasons of state – which the chroniclers readily condone in the progenitor of the race – Vijayo sent Kuveni away to be killed by the *Yakkhas* in another part of the island as a spy. Her two children escaped to the mountains where they married and became the ancestors of the primitive hill tribes, the *Veddhas* of present-day Ceylon.

Meanwhile the envoys to the King of Madura in Southern India returned with the glad news that the request of Vijayo for the hand in marriage of the king's daughter, had been granted. 'And the king of Madura sent his daughter, bedecked with all her ornaments, and all that was needful for the journey . . . and one hundred maidens as brides for the chief followers of Vijayo . . . elephants withal and horses and waggons worthy of a king, and craftsmen and a thousand families of the eighteen guilds . . . The princess was solemnly consecrated as queen, and Vijayo, the lord of men, forsaking his former evil ways, ruled over all Lanka in peace and righteousness.' (10)

It was the lion ancestor of Vijayo who gave us the name 'Ceylon'. The Sanskrit *Sinha* (lion), with the suffix – *diva* (island), through the variant Senendiva became the Serendib of the Arab merchants, was contracted to Ceilao by the Portuguese, modified to Zeilan or Ceilan by the Dutch, and finally Anglicized to Ceylon.

Within the dense cocoon of fancy spun by the chronicler, the legend of Vijayo preserves the historic fact of the early colonization of the island by an Aryan race from North-Central India, in or about the fifth century B.C. The point of embarkation would appear to have been high on the West-coast of India in Gujerat. The language of the immigrants was Pali, closely related to Sanskrit, and their religion was undoubtedly Brahmanism with an admixture of primitive animistic beliefs.

Initially, political authority seems to have been invested in the clan or village head-man, or *gamani*, who wielded limited authority. Only as the small settlements at the three or four main centres of colonization expanded, and as each became unified under a single chief, and one of these in turn managed to assert himself over the rival chiefs and assumed suzerainty over the whole island, did the concept of kingship as a political institution evolve. The rise to dominance of the settlement at Anuradhapura saw the growth of what was merely another village into the only city on the island.

Anuradhapura was founded by King Pandukabhaya about a century after the arrival of Vijayo. The name derives from Anuradha, a constellation of stars, and *pura* (city). The constellation must, indeed, have been auspicious, for within a century and a half, Anuradhapura had become an important centre, and by the beginning of the Christian Era it ranked as one of the great capitals of the world.

The first centuries of colonization saw successive waves of Aryan immigrants, chiefly from the Gujerat region but with possible sub-waves from Bengal and Orissa. At the same time there was immigration from South-India but, although important, this element was never able to fundamentally alter the basic North-

Indian character of the society. On the other hand, being a continuous migration, the Dravidian or Tamil element could never be completely absorbed within the mainstream of Sinhalese culture.

The Indo-Aryan colonists, from whichever part of the Indo-Gangetic plain they may have come, had had long experience in husbandry. All the new settlements were riverine in character, with rice the staple crop, and cattle breeding also playing an important role in the economy.

The rapid rise of the ancient civilization of Ceylon depended first and foremost on skill in water conservation. A glance at a relief map of Ceylon will make clear the reason why. A great mountainous core rising to a height of over eight thousand feet occupies the centre of the southern half of the island. This intercepts the moisture from the south-west monsoon, and as a consequence the south-west zone of Ceylon and the central mountainous area have a high annual rainfall of 100-200 inches. The northern and eastern plains which slope gradually down from the central core to the sea receive rain only from the north-east monsoon and have a relatively low rainfall of 60-100 inches.

It was in the 'Dry Zone' that the immigrants settled and the ancient civilization arose. The earliest colonists no doubt relied solely on the rather undependable north-east monsoon to cultivate a single annual crop of rice. With the pressure of population due to more intensive colonization, there was a change to the 'wet' method of rice cultivation in paddy fields, and this made a dependable water supply essential.

India has had a knowledge of irrigation methods from very early times. It seems that irrigation by means of channels cut from rivers and the construction of reservoirs originated in Mesopotamia 'and spread westwards and south-eastwards from the Euphrates valley, reaching the Dravidian districts of India possibly before the Aryan invasion of the country, and being transmitted thence to Ceylon'. (11)

Although there are still earlier references to the construction of reservoirs in the chronicles, the oldest which can be identified with certainty is the Abhaya Tank, today known as the Basawak-kulam, at Anuradhapura. The Mahavamsa records its construction by King Pandukabhaya (437-367 B.C.). There are casual references to it throughout the histories – 'always as a reservoir in working order; and it appears to have remained unbreached as long as Anuradhapura was inhabited – that is, for more than 1500 years, a respectable record for a work of such early date.' (12) The embankment of the Basawak-kulam is a little over a mile wide and a maximum of 22 ft. high. When full, the tank is 255 acres in extent.

Impressive though these figures are, they are completely dwarfed by later efforts. There are some ten reservoirs exceeding 4000 acres, including the Maha Kanadara-wewa of 5670 acres, and the uncompleted 'Giant's Tank' which would have had an area of 6400 acres. The lengths of the embankments extended to a maximum of nine miles and the height, in a few instances, to more than fifty feet, while one canal conveying water from a river being 'tapped' for a reservoir is sixty miles long. So renowned were the Sinhalese in this field that in the eighth century a king of Kashmir 'sent to Ceylon for engineers to form a lake' (13).

Only a strong centralized government and an efficient bureaucracy could muster the resources to construct such large reservoir and canal systems and ensure their maintenance and efficient use. There are references to an 'Inspector of Reservoirs'; to officials supervising the distribution of water from the channels to the paddy fields; to the collection of water dues from the landowners, and to penalties for the unauthorized use of reservoir water. A strict time-schedule was enforced on

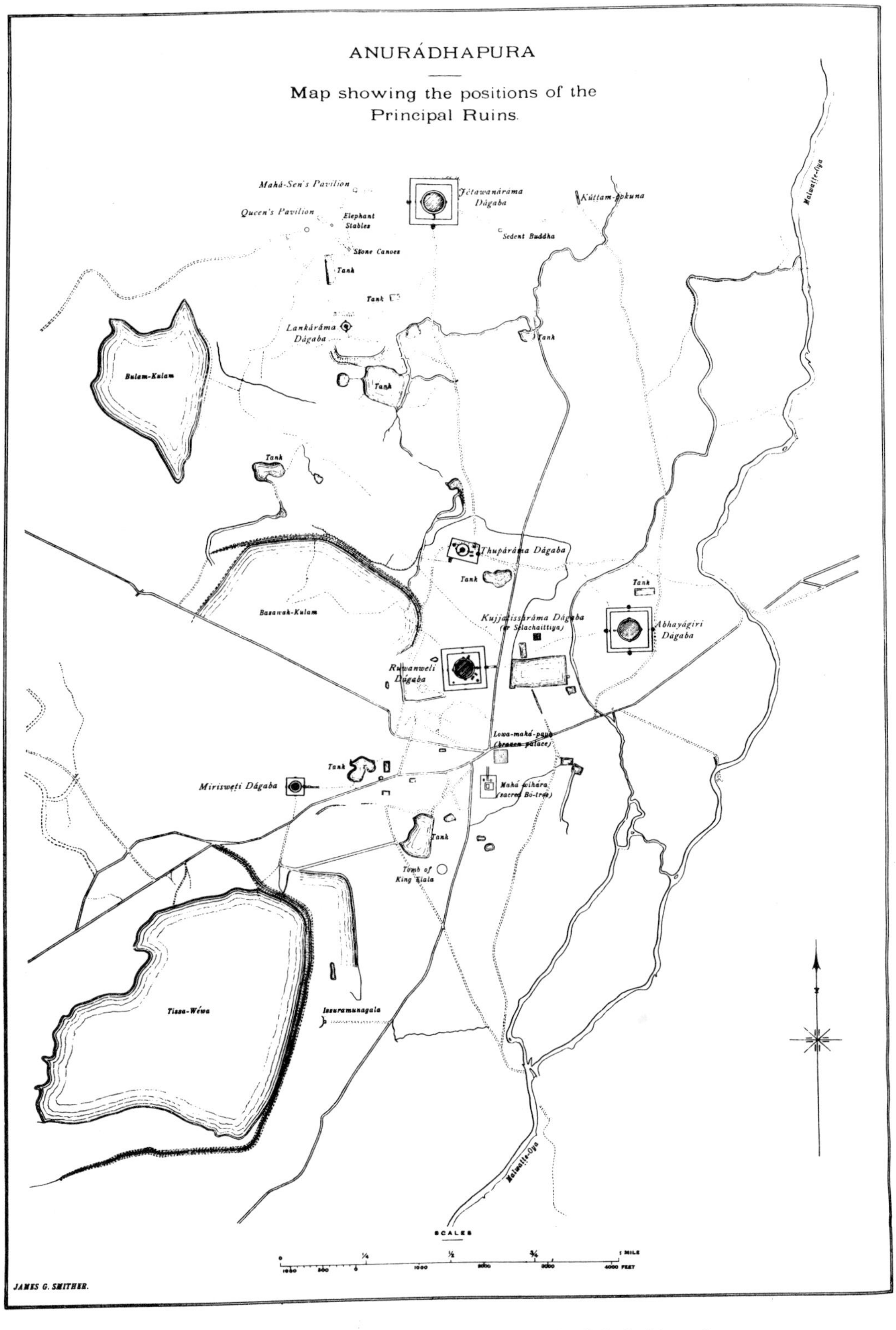

Fig. 2 Map of Anuradhapura, from *Architectural Remains: Anuradhapura*, by J. G. Smither, 1894

cultivators to ensure that all lands fed by a certain channel were ploughed and ready for irrigation when the water was diverted into that channel. Only thus could the available water be used to best advantage.

The design of the reservoirs shows a very thorough knowledge of hydraulic principles. The dams were broad-based to withstand heavy pressures and suitable places were provided for the escape of floodwaters at the ends of the embankment.

Particularly ingenious was the method of regulating the discharge of water from the reservoirs. An inlet culvert, reinforced at its entrance by a high wall serving to support the soil on each side, conducted the water to a rectangular, open well called a *bisokotuva* (14), built near the water level on the embankment. The floor and sides of this well were lined with large stone slabs fitted together with extreme precision to resist the penetration of water under pressure. To this end they were further backed with a thick layer of brick also laid with the greatest care in fine lime mortar burned from coral. The *bisokotuva* housed the wood lock or valve which could be slid vertically in a groove to open or close the discharging culvert. This led from the well to the foot of the outer slope of the bank.

It was only the discovery by Sinhalese engineers of the principle of the 'valve tower' or 'valve pit', more than two thousand years ago – 'rediscovered' and first used again by modern engineers in the middle of the nineteenth century – that permitted them to construct the greatest irrigation works known until modern times.

The knowledge possessed by the tank builders of ancient Ceylon in such fields as trigonometry was astounding. A survey conducted since Independence for the purpose of restoring certain ancient works, merely confirmed that the instruments used for contour levelling must have been virtually as accurate as those available today. The *ellas* or canals which conducted the water from the great central reservoirs to smaller storage tanks and thence to the paddy-fields were, for example, customarily laid to a fall of only one foot per mile; in some instances as little as six inches per mile.

The most decisive event in the long history of Ceylon took place during the reign of King Devanampiya Tissa (307-267 B.C.) namely the island's conversion to Buddhism. King Tissa, 'beloved of the gods', was on friendly terms with the great Emperor Asoka, who bears the same relationship to Buddhism as Constantine does to Christianity.

Ruling an empire extending over the greater part of India, the Emperor's conversion gave to Buddhism the prestige of a State Religion and all the benefits of royal patronage. It also set in motion one of the most effective proselytizing campaigns in history as the Emperor sent missionaries throughout his territories and even to neighbouring lands.

The mission to Ceylon was headed by the *thera* (elder) Mahinda, who, according to Sinhalese tradition was the Emperor's own son. The meeting of Mahinda and King Tissa took place on the hill of Mihintale some ten miles from Anuradhapura. When he had presented his credentials, the *thera* subjected the king to an intelligence test.

'What name does this tree bear, O King?'

'It is called a mango.'

'Is there yet another mango beside this?'

'There are many mango-trees.'

'And are there yet other trees besides this mango and the other mangoes?'

'There are many trees besides this mango and the other mangoes.'

'And are there besides the other mangoes and those trees which are not mangoes yet other trees?'

'There is this mango-tree.'

Having thus ascertained that the king was capable of logical reasoning, Mahinda

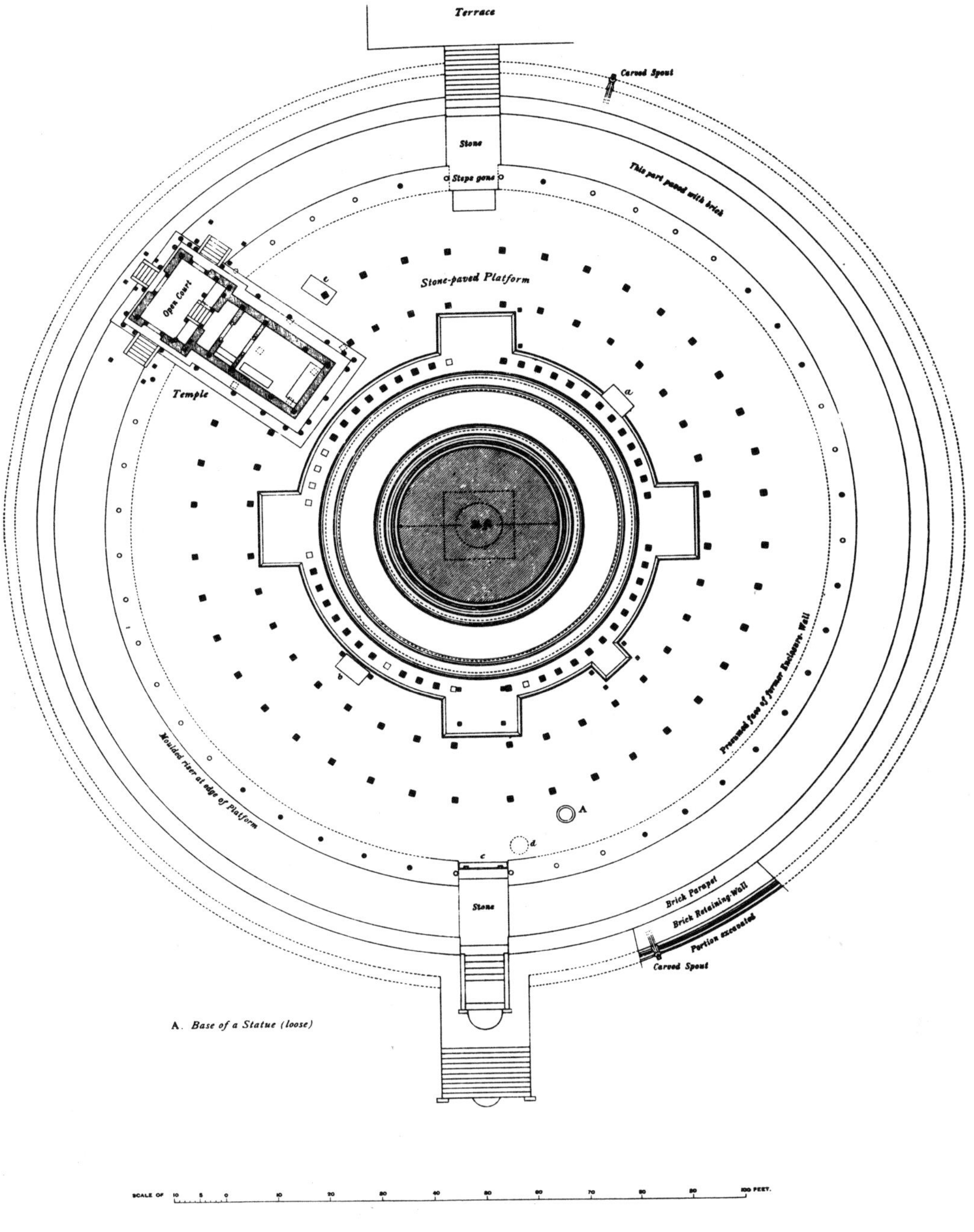

Fig. 3 Plan of the Thuparama Dagoba, Anuradhapura, from *Architectural Remains: Anuradhapura*, by J. G. Smither, 1894

preached the rather abstruse doctrine of the *Culahatthipadupamasuttanta*, or 'Simile of the Elephant's Footprint'. The king was favourably impressed with the sermon and invited Mahinda and his companions to the royal palace where they continued their exposition before a large audience. This was so successful that the royal family and several thousand people were converted and a few even ordained as *bhikkhus* (priests). The *Mahavihara* or 'Great Monastery', (15) which was to become the historic centre of Theravada Buddhism in Ceylon was founded, and a royal pleasance, the Mahamegha Garden, dedicated to the exclusive use of the new faith.

The undoubted precedent for this land grant was the presentation by King

Bimbisara of his own pleasure garden to the Buddha. Not to be outdone by this early benefactor of the Faith, King Tissa deeded no less than twenty square miles within the city limits. 'The superb elephants of state, Mahapaduma and Kunjara were harnessed to a golden plough and the king himself, decked in all the insignia of royalty, accompanied by the *theras* and escorted by the ranks of his army, held the haft of the plough, marking the limits of the consecrated area.' He ploughed the furrow in a circle and 'when the fixing of the boundaries was completed, the great earth quaked'.

A monastery was erected on sacred Mihintale and the rock became riddled with the cells of anchorites. When Fa-Hsien visited Ceylon in the fifth century A.D. there were still two thousand monks living there and also the famous ascetic Dharmagupta of whom he noted: 'He has lived for more than forty years in an apartment of stone, constantly showing such gentleness of heart, that he has brought snakes and rats to stop together in the same room, without doing one another any harm.' (16)

The route from the capital to Mihintale constituted the *Via Sacra* of ancient Ceylon and was the scene of the most splendid processions of the Buddhist hierarchy. It was lined with shrines and monuments, and on several occasions was covered at the command of the king with a carpet for its entire length of eight miles, so that pilgrims who had washed in a sacred pool at Mihintale might reach the capital with feet unsoiled. The road to Mihintale terminated at the foot of a monumental stairway of no fewer than 1840 steps, carved from slabs of granite, except for the topmost 150 steps which were cut from the living rock. Still today streams of barefooted pilgrims tread the well-worn steps lined with an avenue of aged frangipanni. At the time of my visit, the enormous shrubs were in late bloom, the stairs almost hidden in fallen blossom and the scent quite overpowering.

The ashes of the apostle are enshrined in the bell-shaped Ambastala Dagoba – as the Buddhist reliquary-mound or *stupa* is known in Ceylon (17) – surrounded by a grove of coco-nut palms. To combat the effect of the high humidity which quickly discolours white plaster, the stupa has recently been painted aluminium – a practical but aesthetically disastrous solution which we must hope will not become the vogue.

The Thuparama Stupa, rising pristine and elegant on a small knoll in a clearing surrounded by the magnificent old trees of the Mahamegha Garden, is one of the most picturesque and evocative sights of Anuradhapura (Plate 6, and plan, Fig. 3). It is also of the greatest historic importance; for it is the oldest structure standing in either Ceylon or India. It was built by the pious Tissa about 300 B.C. to house two relics of Gautama Buddha, his right collar-bone and his alms-bowl, which the king is said to have obtained from the Emperor Asoka.

The installation of the relics, as described in the Mahavamsa, was attended by a fitting quota of miracles and magic portents. When the sacred relics arrived from India, the king thought to himself 'If this is a true relic of the Sage, then shall my parasol bow down; of itself my elephant shall sink upon its knees, and this relic-urn containing the relic shall descend upon my head . . . and so it came to pass. And as if sprinkled with ambrosia, the monarch was full of joy, and taking the urn from his head, he set it on the back of an elephant. Then did the elephant trumpet joyfully and the earth quaked.' And the elephant, followed by the king and a great throng, left the city by the south gate and eventually stopped 'at a place covered with kadamba-plants and adari-creepers'. On this chosen spot the stupa was built. (18)

10 The Disciple Ananda mourning for the death of Buddha; colossal rock-cut sculpture, Gal Vihara, Polonnaruwa, Ceylon

11/12 Fifth century frescoes at Sigiriya, Ceylon

13 One of the 'Golden Ladies'; fifth century fresco at Sigiriya, Ceylon

14 Enormous lion paws at the entrance to the rock stronghold of the parricide king, Kassapa, Sigiriya, Ceylon

10

I

I

13

14

15

16

18

19

The object of pious reverence for over two thousand years, the Thuparama Dagoba has been periodically enriched and as regularly despoiled: a gold pinnacle was affixed to the spire by King Upatissa II in the 4th Century and removed by Dalupia-Tissa II in the 7th; King Mahinda III donated 'a cover of gold ornamented with bands of silver', in the 8th Century and in the 9th this was carried off by Pandyan invaders from India. It was restored for the umpteenth time in the reign of King Parakrama Bahu I (1157-1186 A.D.) but in the first half of the nineteenth century had reverted to a mound, nearly flat on top and covered with brushwood. It was shown thus by Major Forbes (19) and was in the same state when Sir Emerson Tennent saw it in 1848. It was apparently restored shortly afterwards in its present form, a most elegant, bell-shaped stupa surmounted by a cubical block of brickwork, the *devata kotuwa* or 'citadel of the gods', and a conical ringed spire set upon a cylinder. The dimensions of the Thuparama are modest: a diameter of 31 ft at the springing of the dome of the bell and 40 ft 6 ins at the base, and a height of 55 ft 6 ins to the top of the spire. The lower half, with its mouldings and sculptured decorations, and the platform, on which the stupa stands, are original. So, too, are the four concentric rows of monolithic granite columns, their capitals exquisitely carved with grotesques of dwarfs, horned lions couchant, birds with outstretched wings, and foliate motifs, that surround the stupa and complement its massive bulk with their pencil-thin vertical accents.

Such rows of columns are peculiar to early Sinhalese stupas and their purpose has been hotly debated. The fact that the pillars decrease in height as the circles expand, the innermost ring being 23 ft and the outermost only 14 ft, has prompted the suggestion that they might have supported a roof which extended over the entire stupa (20). In view of the sanctity of the relics such additional protection might well have been deemed desirable. Certainly, the modest size of the stupa would have made it feasible structurally. Another theory is that a roof was erected between a couple of concentric rows only, providing a covered way for ritual circumambulation; yet another that the pillars supported beams from which were suspended painted panels. Whatever additional use they might have served, they certainly supported the festoons of lights and garlands of fragrant flowers which are a feature of all the island's festivals.

Among those inspired by the apostle Mahinda to enter the monastic life were several thousand women, including some members of the royal family. The apostle, however, declared that although he could effect their conversion, only a consecrated priestess could accept their vows. He suggested that his sister, Sanghamitta, or 'Friend of the Order' who had become the prioress of a nunnery at Pataliputra, be prevailed upon to come to Ceylon and institute an order of Buddhist nuns. The minister charged by King Tissa with this mission was further directed to request the Emperor Asoka to allow his daughter to bring with her a branch of the sacred Bo-tree under which the Buddha had achieved enlightenment at Bodhgaya. Both requests were granted: the princess Sanghamitta came and brought a slip of the sacred tree, rooted in a vase of gold. Every stage in the transfer of the sacred relic, as recorded in the minutest detail in the *Mahavamsa*, was effected with the greatest ceremony. When finally planted in the Mahamegha Garden, 'the earth quaked and the roots growing over the brim of the vase, struck down into the earth, closing in the vase. When the great Bodhi-tree had taken its place all the people who had come together from the country around worshipped it with offerings of perfumes and flowers. Then a tremendous cloud drenched the tree with rain, and cool, dense mists enveloped it in a snowy shroud. After seven days the

15 The Lankatilaka Temple (or Buddha – sima – Prasada) and the Kiri Dagoba, Polonnaruwa, Ceylon

16 The Lotus Bath, Polonnaruwa, Ceylon

17 Gateway and 'Moonstone', Watadage, Polonnaruwa, Ceylon

18/19 The Watadage, Polonnaruwa, Ceylon

20 The sage-king, Parakrama Bahu I; colossal rock-cut statue at Polonnaruwa, Ceylon

clouds dispersed and revealed the Bodhi-tree resplendent with a halo of six colours.' And there it stands to this day, more than 2250 years later, the *Jaya Sri Maha Bodinvahanse*, 'the Victorious, Illustrious, Supreme, and Sacred Bo-Tree', object of pious veneration to millions of Buddhists and the oldest historical tree in the world.

The gnarled and twisted giant stands on a terraced platform enclosed by a protective railing. The leaf of the Bo-tree or Pipal (*Ficus religiosa*) is joined to the branch by a very thin stem so that a barely perceptible movement of air causes the leaves to quiver excitedly. The effect of animation is here enhanced by the innumerable strips of cloth with which the devout have draped the railing (21), lending to the picture something of the gay and tawdry picturesqueness of a Neapolitan street scene.

Except for some ancient guardstones with exceptionally fine reliefs of *naga* kings, the surroundings of the tree are relatively modern and of little consequence. Although nothing could be less appropriate, the elaborate main gateway, some hundred and fifty years old, and of almost comic pompousness, has the wayward charm of some gauche Victorian outrage. It is the worshippers who invest the scene with its almost palpable atmosphere of sanctity with their restrained cheerfulness, dignity and very real devotion.

There can be little doubt that the sacred Bo-tree at Anuradhapura is that planted by the missionary-princess. Throughout the chronicles there are references to ceremonies held in honour of the Sacred Tree and to matters connected with its preservation. Such a disaster as its death would have been well-nigh impossible to conceal. And if we accept the tree as that planted by Sanghamitta, there is every reason to believe further that it was grown from a shoot obtained from the original Bo-tree, for this tree is known to have been still alive and revered at the time of the Emperor Asoka, and Bodhgaya was within his domains (22).

That the Bo-tree survived the depredations of successive Tamil invasions is due to a happy coincidence: the *Ficus religiosa* is also sacred to the Hindus. Now, alas, even the Holy Tree is succumbing to one of the Buddhas 'unavoidable ills'. It is at last dying of old age.

Below the bund of the Tissawewa, largest of the great 'tanks' at Anuradhapura, stands the rock-cut Isurumuniya Vihara dedicated by the same king (Plate 4). Here to a granite outcrop dramatically fissured on one side have been appended various excrescences: a cosy little 'planter's colonial' porch, stairs, railings, terraces, a belvedere, etc. Add to these a stone-fringed, lotus-dappled pool, just a glimpse of a small white stupa surrounded by tall palms and, above, a white-washed belfry that would not be out of place in a Mediterranean setting, and you have the most extraordinary, yet altogether delightful melange, irresistibly photogenic.

Only rediscovered in the late nineteenth century the temple has become a popular place of pilgrimage and the precincts are always gay with the saffron-coloured robes of the *bhikkhus*.

Inside the temple are some monumental sedent Buddhas. In their gaudy coats of multi-hued enamel, only their noble lines give any inkling of their age. On the terraces outside stand some fine old *dvarapala* guard-stones and a stone relief of a festively-dressed couple seated on a couch, long nicknamed 'The Lovers' (Plate 7).

The chief artistic distinction of Isurumuniya derives from two reliefs carved on the great rock outcrop: one of the Sage Kapila, the other of a trumpeting elephant disporting among lotuses. Carved with enormous vitality in such low relief as to constitute virtually an outline drawing, this has been positioned on the vertical rock surface so that the lower half of the elephant is below the water-line and he

21 Enthroned Buddha; rock-cut Temple of Gal Vihara, Polonnaruwa, Ceylon

22 Frieze of dwarf caryatides in stucco from the Demala Maha Seya or Northern Temple, Polonnaruwa, Ceylon

23 Stucco architectural ornamentation on the façade of the Lankatilaka Temple, Polonnaruwa, Ceylon

24 Bronze image of Avalokitesvara Padmapani from Ceylon. *British Museum, London*

25 Grotesque lion-caryatides in stucco from the Demala Maha Seya or Northern Temple, Polonnaruwa, Ceylon

I

22

23

appears to be bathing in the temple pool – a most effective conceit.

As befits a culture whose very existence depended upon the conservation of water, this element features prominently in the layout of the ancient capital. The great 'tanks' have added immeasurably to the beauty of the natural landscape with their verdant tree-crowned embankments and their vast mirror expanses reflecting the ever-changing pageant of cloud and sky; and they are echoed in miniature by the numerous *pokunas*. These stone-lined pools for ritual ablutions are frequently enhanced by elaborate architectural ensembles of balustrades, stairs and landing-stages, and often, and most fittingly, presided over by finely chiselled steles decorated with five- or seven-headed serpent deities, jealous guardians of the life-giving waters (Plate 2).

Everywhere among the ruins are scattered magnificent specimens of decorative sculpture. Particularly fine are the guardstones with their *dvarapalas* or 'Guardians of the Four Directions', in Ceylon usually in the shape of a *naga* king in human form, attended by a grotesque, pot-bellied dwarf. A seven-headed serpent forms a halo above the rich tiara of the *naga* king and in his upraised hand he holds a 'vase of plenty' sprouting forth prosperity and abundance

Characteristically Sinhalese are the 'moonstones' – and we are referring here not to the milky-blue, semi-precious stone for which Ceylon has also long been famous, but to the semi-circular slab forming a decorative and symbolic termination at the foot of a staircase. Thanks to the Buddhist practice of walking barefoot on sacred ground, the millions of feet that have passed over these 'moonstones' have hardly grazed their elaborately-carved surfaces. Those at Anuradhapura, despite their great age, are remarkably well-preserved and of exceptional beauty. The rich decoration, executed in low relief, follows a standard pattern (see Fig. 6). An outer band of luxuriant foliage is followed by a procession of animals – horse, elephant, humped Brahmini-bull and lion – moving with spirited dash and poise as if in a circus ring. This combination of quadrupeds, always in a fixed order and always moving from left to right, is a constantly recurring theme in Indian art. Of very ancient origin, it is already found on the commemorative pillars of the Emperor Asoka in the third century B.C., and is presumed to symbolize the four quarters of the world. After the animals comes another belt of stylized vegetation, and then a row of *hamsa* or sacred geese dangling flowers in their beaks. The innermost bands are all inspired by the lotus plant, and culminate in stylized lotus petals of exquisite delicacy. The carving throughout combines enormous vitality with perfect restraint. Particularly noteworthy is the skill with which the individual characteristics of each animal have been delineated: the lumbering yet elastic gait of the elephant, so admired in the East; the spirited flash of the horse's hoofs; the waddling gait of the geese; even the supercilious indifference in the eye of the beloved bovine (23) – all have been captured to perfection. The lion alone is unconvincing and, indeed, rather comical, attributable no doubt to the fact that lions were unknown in Ceylon – or India for that matter – and the artists, therefore, depicted them from hearsay.

The Dravidian or Tamil kingdoms of Southern India (24) played an important role in Sinhalese history from a very early date. Vijayo, himself, as we have seen took as his queen a princess of Madura, thus initiating the common practice of dynastic alliances with the royal houses of the mainland.

As devout Buddhists to whom the taking of life was that most to be avoided, the Sinhalese came to rely more and more on Tamil mercenaries. This was to prove disastrous. In 237 B.C. two Tamil adventurers usurped the throne and ruled for

26 A Naga king in human form serving as a Dvarapala or 'Gateway Guardian'. He holds a vase of plenty sprouting forth prosperity and abundance, and is attended by pot-bellied dwarfs; Watadage Polonnaruwa, Ceylon

27 A Dvarapala stands guard at a transverse corridor leading to the inner sanctum of a temple. Note the radiating voussoirs of the arch, flaunting the Indian prohibition of 'the arch that never sleeps'; Pagan, Burma

28 Buddha image in the Htilominlo Temple, Pagan, Burma

29 Colossal gilded Buddha in the Ananda Temple, his hands raised in the symbolic gesture of the Dharmachakra Mudra, representing 'The Turning of the Wheel of the Law', Pagan, Burma

22 years, and ten years later the first full-scale Tamil invasion came under a Cholyan prince named Elara who ruled as King of Lanka for forty-four years. Although a Hindu, he protected the national religion, undertook new enterprises and good works and acquired a legendary reputation for impartial justice. He is said to have had a bell at the head of his bed with a long rope attached, which could be rung by anyone who sought justice. One legend relates that Elara's son, while driving in his chariot along the bund of the Tissa-wewa, accidentally drove over a calf. The mother-cow promptly went and rang the bell and when King Elara had heard her story, he condemned his son to have his neck broken with the same wheel that had passed over the calf's neck!

In the wild Rohuna country beyond the Mahawelliganga River, several native princes held petty court, all acknowledging the suzerainty of King Elara. One of these princes, a grandson of the great Devanampiya Tissa, had two sons, Gamini and Saddha-Tissa. While still boys, their father placed three portions of rice before them and made them swear as they ate the first to uphold the *Sangha* or community of monks; as they ate the second portion, never to dispute among themselves, and lastly, never to take up arms against the Tamils. They readily agreed to the first two clauses but angrily threw away the rice rather than swear to the third. The elder boy, Gamini, then went and curled up in bed in a cramped position, and when his mother asked him why he did not stretch himself out comfortably, replied 'How can I, confined as I am in so small a space between Tamils beyond the Mahawelliganga and the ocean'. Obviously a boy born to throw off the yoke of the invader!

When only sixteen, Gamini mustered a small force, and with his ten boon companions – who occupy the same position in Sinhalese history as the Knights of the Round Table – announced his intention of attacking the Tamils. His father forbade the project and Gamini in a fit of pique sent him a woman's jewel to wear. This deliberate insult sent Gamini fleeing for his life to the mountains and earned him the nickname *duttha* meaning 'undutiful'. He was known henceforth as Dutthagamini (25). Only on his father's death did he return from exile to find that his brother had 'seized the queen-mother and the state elephant' and assumed power. A war between the two brothers ensued, ending in a victory for Dutthagamini and a reconciliation. Henceforth, Saddha-Tissa remained loyal to his brother.

The epic struggle during which Dutthagamini subdued one of Elara's strongholds after the other, made the warrior king the national hero of the Sinhalese and inspired one of the liveliest passages of the *Mahavamsa*.

During the assault on the key fortress of Vijitanagara, the defenders poured down molten pitch on the attacking elephants. Kandula, Dutthagamini's favourite elephant – and a household word in Ceylon to this day – fled in agony and plunged into a nearby pool. 'This is no drinking bout (literally *sura*-draught, an intoxicating drink); go batter down the iron gate!' Thus chided, 'the best of elephants proudly took heart, reared himself out of the water and stood defiantly on firm ground. The elephant physician washed the pitch away and put on balm, and he was fed with the choicest fodder and armoured with seven layers of buffalo-hide covered with a skin soaked in oil. Then the king mounted the elephant and cheered him with the words "To thee, dear Kandula I give the lordship over the whole of Lanka". Kandula trumpeted like thunder and, fearless of danger, stormed the gate, pierced its panels with his tusks and trampled the threshold until gate and lintel crashed loudly to the ground.'

Finally after fifteen years of fighting, Dutthagamini met Elara outside

30 Cramped image of the Buddha entering NIRVANA in the Manuha Temple, symbolizing the discomfort of the captive King Manuha who entreated the Enlightened One 'Whithersover I migrate in the endless round of birth and rebirth, may I never again be conquered by another!' Pagan, Burma

31 Sikhara or spire of the Mahabodhi Temple, Pagan, Burma

32 Sulamani Temple, Pagan, Burma

31

32

33

Anuradhapura and challenged him to single combat. The two leaders, each mounted on his war-elephant, armed with javelins and watched by the two armies, engaged in an Homeric struggle which ended in the death of both Elara and his steed. The Tamil army thereupon surrendered and the long war was over.

In a most chivalrous gesture Dutthagamini ordered that the slain leader be accorded all honour. His body was cremated and a tomb erected on the spot where he had fallen. Dutthagamini further directed that from that time forth any procession passing the tomb should 'silence their music and even the princes dismount' as a token of respect. These instructions seem to have been faithfully observed through the centuries. As late as the nineteenth century, the ailing Kandyan chieftain, Pilame Talawe, fleeing after his unsuccessful revolt against the British, got down from his litter and walked a long distance, until he was quite sure he had passed the tomb, at that time overgrown by the jungle.

King Dutthagamini (161-137 B.C.) seems to have been obsessed with the huge loss of life incurred in overthrowing Tamil rule, and devoted much of his reign to pious works calculated to expiate his guilt.

Near the Temple of the Bo-Tree a forest of slender, lichen-flecked granite monoliths some twelve feet high pierces the sward, conjuring up an hallucinatory vision of the bed of nails of some Brobdingnagian ascetic or, more prosaically, the bombed-out assembly-line of some vast, modern factory with row upon row of evenly spaced columns stretching in a dizzy perspective, 1400 in all, covering an area of 250 feet square. The structure of which these monoliths are the sole remains was anything but prosaic: no less than the fabulous *Lohopasada* or 'Brazen Palace'. This was built by King Dutthagamini to house the monks of the Mahavihara, the most important monastic community at Anuradhapura. So determined was the king to acquire the maximum merit from his good work, that he expressly forbade any work to be done without reward and set aside as payment, 'at each of the four gates, eight *lacs* of gold, a thousand bundles of garments, and pitchers filled with ball-sugar, oil, sugar-dust and honey'. Several amusing incidents are cited of persons surreptitiously contributing a single brick or some such trifle, being found out and forcibly paid.

The Lohopasada rose to a height of nine storeys, a veritable sky-scraper apartment-house, with accommodation graded according to rank, the uppermost floors being reserved for the most senior ecclesiastics. Rising to a height of 150 ft at the most conservative estimate, the Lohopasada was covered outside with plates of burnished copper, which shone like gold in the sun, hence its name, 'Brazen Palace'. As befitted the avowed model, a 'Flying Palace', or a celestial palace of the gods, the decor within was of the utmost magnificence. Each of the hundred apartments on each floor had a window 'decorated with ornaments bright as eyes', and was finished in silver, with details further embellished with gems, and with tinkling festoons of gold. The furnishings were no less sumptuous; couches, chairs and carpets alike were of the highest quality and the very rinsing vessel and its ladle were of gold.

The *pièce de résistance* was a pavilion on the ground floor supported by pillars of gold and housing the throne of the chief of the *Tirunansis* (26). This was 'of ivory with a seat of mountain-crystal and with the ivory back further embellished with designs of the sun in gold, the moon in silver, the stars in pearls and lotus-blossoms fashioned of various gems. On the throne was placed an exquisite flabellum wrought from ivory and above stood a white parasol. It had a coral foot, a silver staff and from its edge were suspended rows of little silver bells . . . Palace, parasol,

33 Guardian Lion and the newly re-gilded Shwezigon Pagoda, enshrining a tooth of the Buddha, Pagan, Burma

34 Decorative window of the Myinkaba Kubyaukkyi Temple in typical 'Mon' style, Pagan, Burma

throne and pavilion were beyond price' (27).

The columns we see today were probably not even those of the lowest of the nine floors, but rather of the basement. The superstructure was undoubtedly of wood and as such was particularly vulnerable to destruction and decay. During the following reign it accidentally caught fire from a lamp and was rebuilt with seven storeys. This was later reduced to five storeys, and in the third century A.D. the whole building was dismantled by the apostate King Mahasena to enrich the monastery of a rival sect. Today only the 1400 weatherbeaten monoliths remain to testify to the glory that was the 'Brazen Palace'.

The Ruanweli, or 'Gold Dust' Dagoba, was King Dutthagamini's other major architectural achievement (Plate 8 and Fig. 5). This is a stupa no less than 254 ft in diameter, rising to a height of 180 ft, though at one stage a spire of more attenuated design may well have reached 300 ft. Built of solid brickwork it is set upon a raised platform 475 ft square. As the first of the truly enormous stupas, it so fired the imagination of the Sinhalese that when, later, even larger stupas had been erected, it was still always referred to as the 'Mahathupa' or 'Great Stupa'. Thanks to this primacy, we have a more detailed account of its construction than of any other ancient building in either Ceylon or India. Every precaution was taken to ensure a firm foundation for the mountain of brickwork to come. The soil was dug out to a great depth 'and round stones crushed with hammers were placed in position . . . and stamped down by great elephants whose feet were bound with leather'. Upon this base were laid successive layers of clay, brick and cement and over this a network of iron 'sprinkled with sweet-scented marumba'. More layers of metal and stone followed and, finally, the *pièce de résistance*: 'A plate of silver cemented in red arsenic dissolved in sesamum-oil.' Even without this last flight of the Chronicler's fancy (?), the work was well and truly done, for under a load comparable to that of an Egyptian pyramid, the foundations have showed no sign of settlement after two thousand years.

The laying of the foundation stone was an occasion of the utmost magnificence. Dignitaries from the far corners of the Buddhist world attended, and, lest the appearance of the populace disgrace the solemnity of the occasion, the king 'placed at the four gates of the city many barbers and servants for the bath and for cutting the hair, clothes likewise and fragrant flowers'. Then the king decked in robes of state, accompanied by his ministers and surrounded by a throng of dancing and singing maidens 'richly clothed like celestial nymphs', came to the stupa and after many ceremonies 'laid the first foundation stone upon the sweet-smelling clay and offered jasmine flowers'.

When the king asked the master-builder what shape he proposed for the stupa, 'the master-builder had a golden bowl filled with water, and he took some water in his hand and let it fall on the surface of the water. And a great bubble arose, like unto a half-globe of crystal. And the master-builder said 'Thus will I make it'. Then was the king well-pleased and bestowed on him a rich garment, a pair of ornamented slippers and twelve thousand *Kahapanas* (square copper coins).

In the centre of the relic chamber the king placed a jewelled Bo-Tree. The stem was of pure silver, the fresh leaves glittered with gems, the withered leaves were wrought in gold and the fruits and tender shoots were of coral. Around the foot of the tree were arranged rows of vases containing 'the four perfumed waters' and flowers fashioned of all kinds of jewels, while overhead was suspended a gorgeous canopy fringed with a network of pearls and hung with little tinkling golden bells. At each of the four sides of the chamber there was a small golden statue of the

35 Enormous gilded Buddha image in the interior of the Ananda Temple, Pagan, Burma

36 Gilded and painted stone relief in the circumambulatory corridor of the Ananda Temple, showing Queen Mahadevi, Mother of the Buddha, borne by attendants, setting out on her journey; Pagan, Burma

35

36

37

38

39

Buddha seated on a throne. Representations of the eight auspicious signs and 'rows of four-footed beasts and geese'; the same motif as on the moonstones, no doubt, figured prominently in the decoration.

When the time had come to transfer the relics to the great stupa, 'the king, glad at heart, well versed in the duties of kings, arrayed in all his ornaments, passed around the stupa three times, going towards the left (28), climbed up on the east side, and then descended into the relic chamber' and enshrined the relics. Above the main chamber a second was formed where any who wished could deposit jewels to the glory of the relics . . . And when all was complete, two novice monks charged with the task, solemnly closed the relic chamber 'with a fat-coloured stone' – a phrase evoking all the opulence and beauty of the 'mutton fat' jades of Imperial China.

The building was not yet completed when King Dutthagamini fell sick. The *Mahavamsa* has a touching account of the dying king being carried on a palanquin to a spot from which he could view his two greatest monuments, the Lohopasada and the Ruanweli. His favourite priest, who had formerly been a great warrior and fought beside the king in numerous battles, was at his side and tried to comfort him by having a scribe read an enumeration of the king's many pious deeds. Cited, together with the enormous amounts expended on the building of ninety-nine vihards, etc., is the gift by the king of two precious earrings to provide 'a goodly dish of sour millet-gruel' for five ascetics during a great famine, and the 'provision at eighteen places, of special diets and medicines for the sick, as prescribed by the physicians'. When the account was through, the king turned to his friend and said 'In times past I engaged in battle supported by thee; now singlehanded I have commenced my conflict with death, a foe I cannot conquer'. And having charged his brother, Saddha-Tissa to complete the Great Stupa, 'stinting nothing', the great ruler fell silent (29).

Like the Thuparama Dagoba, the Ruanweli has suffered from alternate attempts at restoration followed by renewed destruction as Sinhalese power waxed and waned. However, the very size of the Ruanweli which ensured its survival, also enormously increased the problem of maintenance, and by the early half of the nineteenth century it had been reduced to a wooded hillock some two hundred feet high. In such early photographs as those by Henry Cave, taken in 1896, only the pinnacle of a spire protruding above the highest trees and a band of brickwork around the very lowest portion of the bell betray the fact that this is not a work of nature. The restored band of brickwork was the work of enthusiastic pilgrims, exhorted by the local priest, who it would seem were engaged on a hopeless task. It was considered thus by Cave who observes that 'the race that could make these immense shrines what they once were has vanished, and with it the conditions which rendered such works possible'. He would be surprised to see the Ruanweli today, its enormous bulk at last completely restored, presiding white and majestic over the landscape – symbol of a resurgent and independent East which, to the nineteenth-century Empire builder, must have seemed equally incredible.

The stupa and the pyramid are mankind's two greatest expressions of the tomb. Both derive ultimately from the tumulus of earth raised over the dead; both symbolize to perfection the appropriate qualities of dignity, permanence, protection and repose, coupled with a hint of aspiration. It is significant that the East should have stylized the tumulus in the rounded shape of the stupa with its strong overtones of the organic forms of nature, while the West expressed the same concept within the framework of the stark geometry of the square and the straight line – the

37 Gilded and painted stone relief in the circumambulatory corridors of the Ananda Temple, depicting the father of the Buddha showing his infant son to the learned ascetic, Kaladevala; Pagan, Burma

38 The Gawdawpalin Temple, Pagan, Burma

39 The Dhammayazika Pagoda, Pagan, Burma

Fig. 4 An overgrown stupa at Anuradhapura; engraving from *Eleven Years in Ceylon*, by Major J. Forbes, 1841

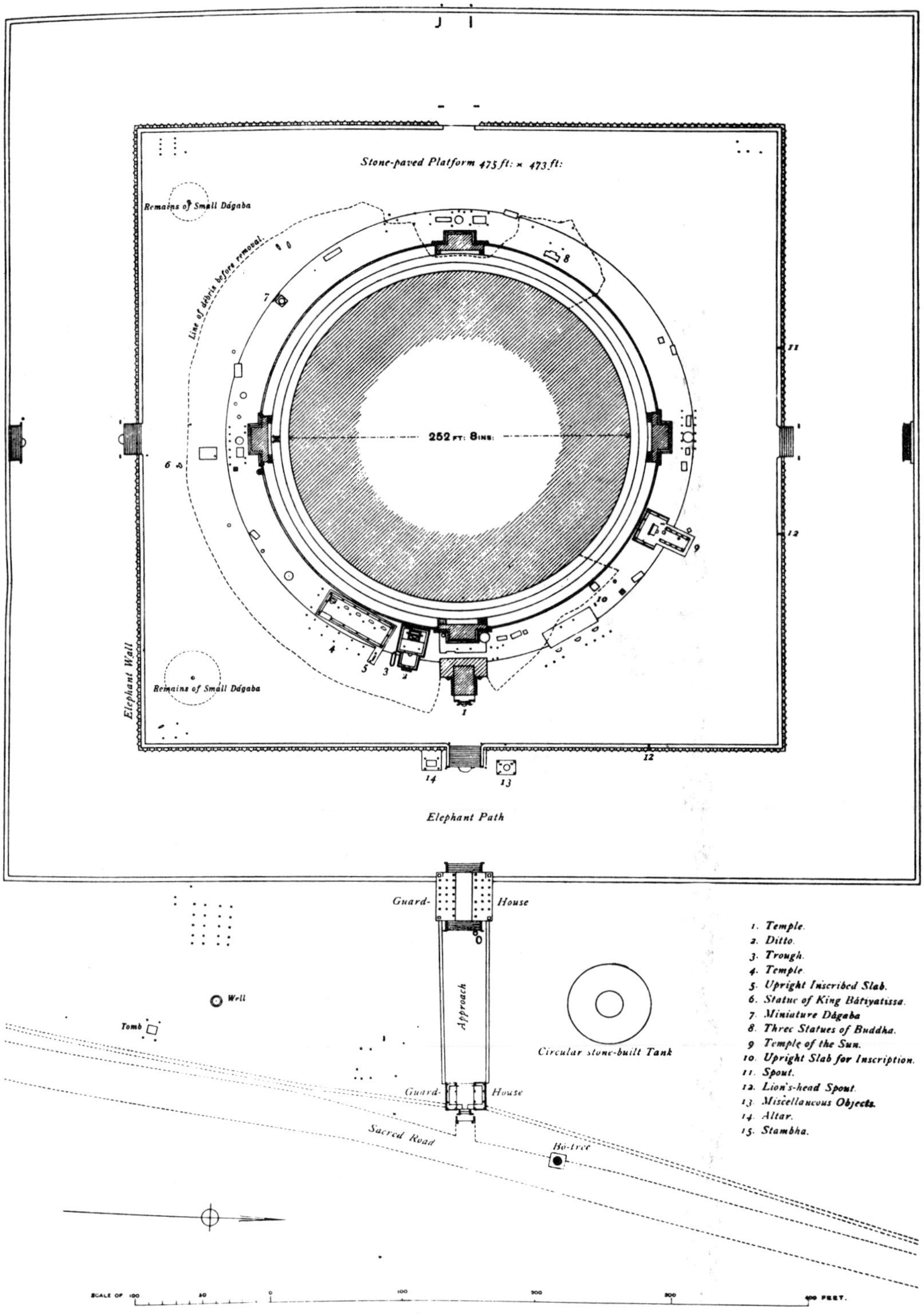

Fig. 5 Plan of the Ruanweli Dagoba, Anuradhapura, from *Architectural Remains: Anuradhapura*, by J. G. Smither, 1894

former stressing the East's sense of 'oneness' with nature, the latter the West's conquest of nature through the power of the human intellect.

During the reign of King Vattagamini (89-76 B.C.), Saddha-Tissa's son, one of the most important events in the annals of Buddhism and in the religious literature

Fig. 6 Sculptured 'Moonstone' threshold, Anuradhapura

of the world took place in Ceylon: the Canonical teachings of the Buddha, which until this date had been transmitted orally, were committed to writing for the first time. This became the orthodox version of the Hinayana Doctrine, invested with supreme authority, and added immeasurably to Ceylon's prestige in the Buddhist world. It was to make copies of certain of these scriptures that the Chinese pilgrim-monk, Fa-hsien, came to Ceylon in 411 A.D. and stayed for two years; and it was from Ceylon that King Manuha of Thaton in Burma obtained copies of 'The True Law' as we shall see later. Ironically, the same King Vattagamini also richly endowed the Abhayagiri Monastery which was the seat of a sect with strong Mahayanist leanings, bitterly opposed by the orthodox Mahavira community.

There are five particularly significant *dagobas* at Anuradhapura: the small but elegant Thuparama and the four giants. Of these we have already discussed the Ruanweli at length. Also dating from King Dutthagamini's reign is the smaller, but still major Mirisweti Dagoba (30), today a pudding-bowl shaped mass of brickwork glowing in every shade of orange and umber, which we must fervently pray escapes restoration. Although the superstructure has gone, the *wahalkadas* or frontispieces facing the four cardinal points are in a reasonable state of preservation and are celebrated for their fine proportions and decorative sculpture.

The Abhayagiri Dagoba, built by Vattagamini, was enlarged by Gajabahu I in the second century A.D. to a height of some 280 ft – greater even than the Ruanweli. With its customary solid core of brickwork, it contains, according to Tennent, enough bricks to build an ordinary railway tunnel twenty miles long, or a wall one foot in thickness and ten feet high from London to Edinburgh (31).

Largest of all the completed stupas (32) of Ceylon is the Jetavana Dagoba, built by King Mahasena, last of the rulers of the *Mahavamsa* or 'Greater Dynasty' in the 4th century A.D. This colossus is 325 ft in diameter and stands on a platform no less than eight acres in extent. Estimates of the height of the original spire range to 400 ft – considerably higher than St. Paul's Cathedral – while the bulk of the Jetavana compares with that of the third pyramid of Gizeh. Both the Abhayagiri and the Jetavana dagobas are still unrestored (33).

Sigiriya

The Rock Fortress of the Parricide King

The fifth century provided Ceylon with the most extraordinary episode in her long history and bequeathed a major legacy to world art.

King Dhatusena was one of the hero-kings who periodically drove out the Tamil invaders. It was he who entrusted the learned sage, Mahanamo, who had been his tutor as a young man, to compile and edit the ancient chronicles and bring them up to date. The *Mahavamsa* and the early part of the *Culavamsa* are from Mahanamo's hand. Although a pious king who undertook numerous good works, Dhatusena seems to have had a particularly unmanageable temper – even by the lax standards of the Sinhalese monarchs. While building the bund of the magnificent Kaluwewa Tank, the work was held up by a holy man deep in meditation, who refused to move. In a fit of rage the king ordered work to proceed and the ascetic was buried alive.

The king had two sons, the elder, Kassapa, by a wife of inferior rank, the younger, Moggallana, by a royal consort. He also had a daughter 'dear to him as his life'. On his sister's son he bestowed the dignity of *senapati* or commander-in-chief of the Army, and gave him his daughter's hand in marriage (34). One day this daughter came to the king, complaining that her husband had beaten her cruelly at the instigation of his mother – a plausible enough allegation in the East where a man's first loyalty remains to his parents, not his wife. When the king saw the weals on his daughter's body, he went berserk and had the meddlesome mother-in-law, his own sister, burned to death. Powerless to avenge her death directly, the general incited Kassapa to usurp the throne. '... And Kassapa raised the umbrella of dominion and destroyed the people who sided with his father, having every scoundrel as his comrade.' King Dhatusena was taken prisoner and walled-up alive, but Kassapa failed in his attempt on the life of his half-brother who escaped to India.

Secure in power, but with a constant foreboding of Nemesis, King Kassapa abandoned the great capital of Anuradhapura and converted a solitary, sheer monolith of granite, rising five hundred feet from the forests of the central plain, into an impregnable fortress-palace. The sole approach to Sigiriya – or the Lion Rock – is by a narrow pathway clinging precariously to a ledge of the beetling cliffs as it winds its way to a plateau half-way to the summit. From here a further flight of steps continues upward between the brick paws of a gigantic lion, all that remains of a figure on the scale of the Sphinx (Plate 14). On the four acres at the summit Kassapa built a splendid palace from which he ruled Ceylon for eighteen years, until Moggallana returned from India with an avenging army. Long years of fear and guilt must surely have destroyed the parricide king's will to live. How else explain his decision to leave his impregnable stronghold, which could laugh a siege to scorn, and meet his brother on equal terms on the plain below? Fate was against him. In the ensuing battle he was forced to turn his elephant to avoid swampy ground and his followers, interpreting this as a sign of retreat, fled. The battle was lost and Kassapa committed suicide. Shortly afterwards, Sigiriya was

40 The Buddha in his five-storied palace before the 'Great Renunciation'; gilded and painted relief in the Ananda Temple, Pagan, Burma

41 Grotesque, decorating the Sulamani Temple at Minnanthu, Pagan, Burma

42 Ogres disgorging chaplets of pearls, stucco ornamentation of the Myinkaba Kubyaukkyi Temple, Pagan, Burma

41

42

abandoned. Today only the foundations of the palace, extending to the very brink of the precipice, and the great water cisterns, hewn in part from the living rock, remain on the summit.

The great attraction of Sigiriya is to be found in a rock pocket some forty feet above the access pathway: a gallery of almost life-sized beauties in fresco which are among the best-preserved treasures of ancient painting (jacket front and plates 11, 12 and 13). The twenty-two figures which survive, originally formed part of a monumental scheme of decoration of several hundred. This was so famous that for centuries after Sigiriya had been abandoned, visitors still came from all over Ceylon to see 'The Golden Ones'. This, and the most personal reactions of the visitors, we know thanks to one of mankind's generally most disagreeable – and seemingly universal – habits: scribbling on walls. The surface chosen for this invaluable act of vandalism at Sigiriya was, fortunately, not the paintings, but the mirror-smooth plastered inner face of the high parapet wall of the access gallery.

The physical charms of the ladies are extolled with a poetic ardour rare, indeed, among vandals.

Sweet girl,
Standing on the mountain,
Your teeth are like jewels,
Lighting the lotus of your eyes.
Talk to me gently of your heart.
Who is not happy when he sees
Those rosy palms, rounded shoulders,
Gold necklaces, copper-hued lips
And long long eyes?
        or yet again
The girl with golden skin
Enticed the mind and eyes.
Her lovely breasts
Caused me to recall
Swans drunk with nectar (35).

The one thing these comments do not tell us, apparently because these early visitors themselves did not know, is who these ladies represent. Bell, the first archaeologist to give a detailed account of the frescoes, declared they were the wives of King Kassapa. Another theory, based on the fact that the figures are cut off below the waist by clouds, is that they are *apsarases* or celestial nymphs, while Dr Paranavitana maintains that the plan of Sigiriya as a whole was devised as a symbolic representation of the Paradise of Kuvera, the God of Riches who dwelt among the clouds on the summit of Mount Kailasa, and that the ladies are 'Lightning Princesses' attended by 'Cloud Damsels'. Whether celestial symbols of sensual gratification or idealized ladies of the court fulfilling the same function in the here and now, the ladies are the embodiment of female charm. The nubile breasts, full hips and tiny waists conform perfectly to accepted Indian canons of beauty. Peculiarly Sinhalese, however, is the hieratic gravity of the gestures and the suggestion of aloof detachment which provide the perfect foil to their almost overpowering physical attributes. If celestial maidens, they are probably scattering blooms in honour of the Buddha. This practice of *puja* has continued to the present day. Women still bear platters of blossoms to the temples with precisely the same gestures as the dark-skinned serving maids or 'cloud damsels' of Sigiriya.

43 Stucco ornamentation of the Hsutaungpyi Monastery, Pagan, Burma

44 The gilded cupola of the Ananda Temple, Pagan. *Height* 180 *feet*

Flowers play a greater role in Buddhist services than in those of any other religion and nowhere is this more true than in Ceylon. The *Rajaratnacari* chronicle records a daily offering at one temple alone of one hundred thousand blooms – each day a different flower – and during the reign of King Batiya Tissa at the time of Christ, the entire surface of the Ruanweli Dagoba was on one occasion festooned with jasmine from base to pinnacle and special machinery erected to keep the blooms watered.

One of the delights in store for the visitor to any of the temples of Ceylon is that even when a shrine is specially unlocked by the guardian, he is greeted not by the expected smell of dank decay but by the sweet fragrance of freshly-plucked flowers – the purple and greenish-white lotus, symbol of purity and flower of Buddhism, dominating the riotous profusion of blooms lovingly arranged before the images.

Should the Golden Ladies of Sigiriya represent ladies of the court, the presence of flowers in the composition has all the more intriguing, erotic overtones. Women are frequently likened to plants and flowers in Indian literature and the very act of fondling a blossom in the presence of the beloved is a conventional sign of willingness to surrender to his advances.

Thus it is construed by the visitor who writes:

The golden-coloured ones
Sign to me with their flowers.
Since she held flowers in her hand,
My passion was aroused,
Her body catching my eyes
As she stood in silence (36).

Many lament the silence and 'stony-hearted indifference' of the maids:

We spoke
But they did not answer.
Those ladies of the mountain,
They did not give us
The twitch of an eye-lid (37).

'Are they human or divine?' To one visitor at least, their very silence proves their divinity conclusively. 'Had they been women, could they possibly have remained silent so long!'

Stylistically the paintings may be regarded as an off-shoot of the great Gupta school of mural painting whose chief surviving masterpieces are to be found in the Ajanta Caves. In contrast to those monumental and highly stylized compositions, the paintings of Sigiriya are far simpler – even a trace provincial, if you like – but also far more spontaneous and free in their execution and, therefore, to modern eyes, perhaps all the more appealing in the same way that Rubens' sketches so often delight us more than his paintings.

45 Jataka illustrating a scene from a previous incarnation of the historic Buddha; glazed terra-cotta plaque from a terrace of the Mingalazedi Pagoda, Pagan, Burma

46 Fresco cycle in the Wetkyi – in Temple, illustrating scenes from previous incarnations of the Buddha; Pagan, Burma

47 Terra-cotta plaque illustrating the Jataka tale of the Decoy Partridge in the Petleik Pagoda, Pagan, Burma

45

46

4

Polonnaruwa

Late Flowering of a Great Tradition

The history of ancient Ceylon followed a seemingly inexorable cycle, repeated time and again. A period of efficient native administration, marked by great industry and prosperity would be followed by a palace revolution, assassinations, a disputed succession or some other civil commotion: a debilitating struggle between the various factions would ensue, and into the breach – sometimes on the pretext of raising a particular claimant to the throne, on other occasions quite unabashedly in search of booty – would step the Tamil invader. Hopelessly weakened by their internecine struggles and, as often as not, unable even to present a united front to the invader, the Sinhalese would be routed and a Tamil would usurp the throne. This occupation would continue until, seemingly as inevitably, a Sinhalese warrior-prince would muster resistance and sweep from the safety of the mountain fastnesses, to which, surprisingly, the writ of the conquerors seems never to have extended. With the return of a stable regime a period of prosperity would follow, then more civil strife and the whole weary cycle would be repeated.

After the death of Moggallana who, it will be recalled, himself came to the throne with the help of an Indian army, the situation deteriorated rapidly. The periods of independence became less frequent, and those of foreign rule even more disastrous, for there was a significant change in the nature of the Tamil occupations. Whereas the earlier usurpers generally ruled well enough and respected the rights of the Buddhist community – a fact readily admitted even by the partisan chroniclers in the case of Elara – the later invaders seemed content merely to pillage and destroy. The early clashes could in many respects be considered as dynastic rather than racio-religious struggles, but the feud now took on a far more bitter aspect with the *Damilos* or Tamils firmly identified in the national consciousness as the arch-enemies of the Sinhalese people – a legacy of hate which has borne bitter fruit in our own day.

Anuradhapura was sacked time and again and in 781 the Sinhalese in utter desperation abandoned the city which had been their sacred capital for a thousand years and removed to Polonnaruwa (38), sixty miles to the east. Here the Sinhalese raised a splendid new city which, inevitably, attracted the cupidity of the invaders.

During the reign of King Sena I (833-853), Polonnaruwa was sacked by the Pandyans, but a little later the tables were unexpectedly turned. The Sinhalese, espousing the cause of a prince of Madura rebelling against his father, occupied the Pandyan capital, recovered the booty taken from Polonnarawa and installed their protégé as king.

A brief period of fruitful alliance with the ruler of Madura followed during the early tenth century, but this only served to increase the enmity of the rival Cholas then rising to ascendancy in Southern India. The combined Pandyan-Sinhalese army was defeated at the Battle of Vellur and Chola incursions followed. These culminated in the full-scale invasion by the great Chola ruler, Rajavaja I in 993. He and his successors incorporated Ceylon as a province of the Chola Empire until

48 Stucco Decorative Detail, Pagan, Burma

49 The Bodhisattva Padmapani; fresco in the Nandamannya Temple, Pagan, Burma

the Sinhalese reasserted their independence in 1070. Against overwhelming odds Vijayo Bahu I drove out the invaders and during his long reign of forty years, the kingdom recovered from the ravages of the Chola occupation. Unfortunately, Vijayo Bahu I, too, left a disputed succession and there was another protracted struggle for power. It seemed as if all would again be lost, when the most remarkable figure in the whole history of Ceylon stepped on to the stage.

Parakrama Bahu the Great (1157-1186 A.D.) was not in the direct line of succession and his route to the throne was marked by the usual subterfuge and treachery, justified by the chroniclers on the basis of his 'divine fitness to rule'. Once secure upon the throne his reign was, however, a model of able administration, justice and magnanimity. While Vijayo Bahu's signal achievement in rallying his people when their fortunes were at lowest ebb, and expelling the firmly-entrenched usurpers, is somewhat curtly acknowledged in the chronicles – possibly because he was not considered munificent enough towards the Faith – every phase of the career of Parakrama Bahu the Great is recorded in the minutest detail. His uncles were disputing the throne and he was yet but a lad, when he swore to rid his people of the Tamil menace once and for all, and to this end perfected himself in the manly arts of war. He was equally proficient in the sciences and arts: administration, law, religion, logic, rhetoric and music were among his many interests and accomplishments. A sage awareness that the prosperity of his kingdom depended ultimately on the efficient working of the irrigation system, emerges from one of his earliest speeches to his ministers. 'In a country like this not even the least quantity of rain-water should be allowed to flow into the ocean without profiting man . . . Let there not be left anywhere in my kingdom a piece of land, though it be of the smallest dimensions, that does not yield some benefit to man.' He repaired the breached and neglected existing tanks and built a vast new network of canals and reservoirs, including the great *Parakramasamudda* or 'Sea of Parakrama'.

An inscription on a large, granite slab in the Thuparama Temple at Anuradhapura reads: 'His Majesty Parakrama Bahu . . . having made all Lanka's isle to appear like a festive island, having made all Lanka like unto a wishing tree, having made all Lanka like unto an incomparably-decorated house, having subjugated in war the Chola invaders, crossed over to India with great hosts; . . . and kings left their countries and came to him for protection, and he treated them with kindness and stilled their fears; . . . and having met with no rival after his landing, he erected pillars of victory, and returned again to Lanka's isle . . . and having distributed much alms and done much good to the world and to religion, this is the seat on which he sat to allay bodily weariness.' This eulogy is no more than a plain statement of fact. The great Parakrama *did* extend his sovereignty over the entire island of Lanka, making it 'prosperous as a wishing well'; he gave to Polonnaruwa a garland of fine monuments and restored the sacred places of Anuradhapura, then 'overgrown with great trees and the haunts of bears and panthers'; he invaded South India, where his name was held in such awe and respect that his progress was in the nature of a triumphal procession; alone among Sinhalese kings he equipped a navy and undertook successful punitive expeditions against Burma and Thailand in retaliation against interference with Ceylon's elephant trade in these areas.

Parakrama Bahu gave particular attention to the export of gems – a royal monopoly – appointing inspectors to curb graft among the tax officials. Trade flourished during his reign and ships from the far corners of the Orient lay at anchor in the port towns of Ceylon.

50 Celestial spirit in devotional attitude. Fresco from Pagan, Burma

51 Monk telling his rosary beads. Fresco dating from the Mongol occupation of Pagan in the Kyanzittha Cave, Pagan, Burma

52 Colossal head of a demon from a gateway balustrade at Angkor Thom, Cambodia

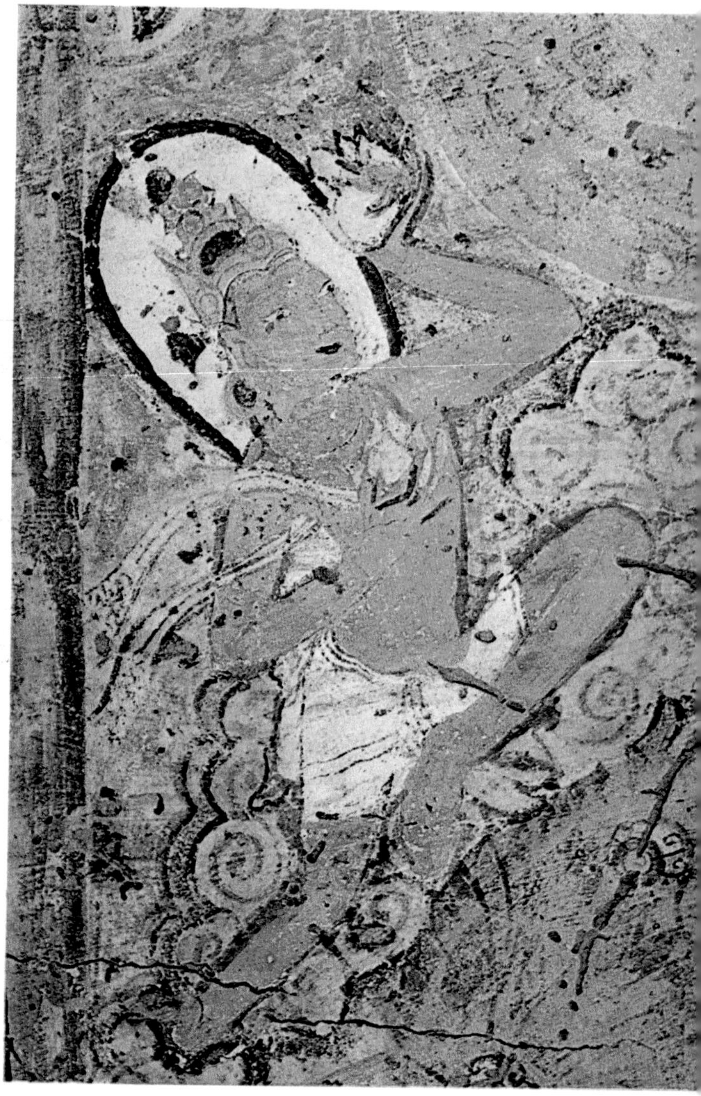

50

51

The Buddhist clergy had fallen on evil days 'sullied by a hundred false doctrines, rent asunder by the schism of the three fraternities and flooded with numerous *bhikkhus* whose sole task was the filling of their bellies.' The king reformed the clergy and even succeeded, where so many of his predecessors had tried and failed, in healing the thousand-year-old schism between the Mahavihara and Abhayagiri factions – a task, the *Culavamsa* informs us, 'twice as onerous as conquering a kingdom'. Although a devout Buddhist, he granted complete freedom of worship, forbade the destruction or desecration of the Hindu temples of the Tamil minority and even built a shrine where the Brahmins might perform their propitiatory rites.

To ensure the protection of his capital against future invaders, Parakrama built a chain of mighty fortifications around the city, their high walls 'gleaming bright as autumn clouds in their coating of lime plaster'. The massive outer ramparts were reinforced by three lesser walls within, and pierced by fourteen gates with such evocative names as The King's Gate, The Lion Gate, The Elephant Gate, and The Garden Gate. Within the walls rose a host of splendid new structures. Not only the usual temples and dagobas – including places of worship for the Hindu minority – but a great variety of secular buildings; accommodations for foreign merchants, who thronged the capital, schools, alms-houses, a theatre, even a hospital, 'well-endowed and staffed with physicians quick at distinguishing the various ailments and well-versed in all the text books.' The king, himself a skilled physician, paid regular visits to the hospital where he not only charmed all with his gracious presence but scrutinized the treatment being administered and where necessary 'indicated the right method . . . and demonstrated the proper use of the instruments by treating patients with his own hand'.

For himself, King Parakrama built a splendid palace seven stories high, lavishly decorated and with hundreds of chambers 'suitable for every season'. Adjoining the palace he laid out a private pleasure-garden planted with exotic-sounding 'bimbijalakas, malati, tamala and navamalika shrubs, with coco-palms and campaka, asoka and tilaka trees, with patali, nipa and sal trees, with mango, jambu and kadamba trees' – all 'twined about with jasmin creepers and filled with the murmur of bees drunk with nectar'.

There were artificial lotus ponds and numerous garden pavilions, one with columns of sandalwood, another octagonal and 'resembling an ear ornament', a third 'with a wreath of serpentine windings' (39). 'The crown jewel of the garden' was a large bath-house resplendent with figures of ivory and evidently equipped with an efficient plumbing system, for we are told that 'a constant shower of water, like to that pouring from a mountain-cloud, flowed from the pipes of the apparatus.'

One of the most beautiful examples of Buddhist architecture remaining in Ceylon or all Asia, for that matter, is the Watadage. This, no doubt, is the building referred to in the *Culavamsa* as 'a beautiful round temple wholly of stone for the Tooth Relic (40), adorned with glorious pillars, staircases and outer walls'. On a large circular platform of shoulder height and plain design rises a far smaller concentric terrace. This has a retaining wall decorated with fine sculptures and surmounted by a parapet wall of pierced stone lattice-work accented at regular intervals with tall pillars of stone. Access to the terrace is by four staircases at the cardinal points. These have moonstone thresholds, and guardstones exceptional for their grace even in Ceylon, terminating side balustrades in the form of the mythical *makara* – that improbable composite of sea-monster and elephant (41). Outstanding as are these reliefs, they are eclipsed in memory by the *pièce de résistance*: the stair risers. Each of these is carved with a running frieze of dwarf Atlantes, minute in scale but

53 Three-headed deity from the 'Gate of Death', Angkor, Cambodia. *Musée Guimet, Paris*

54 Causeway balustrade of gods and triple-crowned south gateway of Angkor Thom, Cambodia

monumental in their vigour, who play at supporting the stone treads. Behind the circular parapet wall, at such a distance as to form a promenade, rises a high circular wall of brick, also broken only at the cardinal points. Within this wall, whose height effectively blocks out the mundane world and focuses attention inwards, runs another spacious concentric terrace permitting ritual circumambulation of the central core: a brick *dagoba* – formerly housing the Tooth Relic – accented at the four cardinal points not by the customary *wahalkada* or stone frontispiece of architectural character, but by four seated Buddhas of ineffable calm, hands folded in the *dhyana mudra* or symbolic gesture of 'inward absorption' (Plates 18 and 19).

The view of the complex from without, with the stairs seeming to pierce successive, concentric barriers until they reach the core of Reality, an Eternal Calm symbolized by the restful hump of the stupa is impressive in the extreme.

Admirable, too, both as an architectural accent and in its symbolism, is the view of the Buddha images at the head of the stairs, presiding unruffled and detached, yet externally vigilant, over the sole means of access to the inner sanctum of the spirit.

Near to the Thuparama temple, a Buddhist structure of marked Hindu character, surmounted by a squat tower and containing, within, the slab inscribed with the eulogy of King Parakrama, stands a most curious little building, the Sat-mahal-pasada. This diminutive step-pyramid of seven tiers so far resembles the great temple-mountains of Angkor in concept as to have elicited the theory that it was for the use of Cambodian merchants or mercenaries in the employ of the Sinhalese ruler, and there is, indeed, a contemporary reference to the area of the city in which it is located as the 'Cambodian quarter'.

Unique to Polonnaruwa is the romantic *Nissanka-lata-mandapaya* or 'Hall of the Flower-Trail of King Nissanka', popularly called the 'Floral Altar'. Ranged around a diminutive stupa on a raised stone terrace surrounded by a stone-fence or rail, are eight curious, twisted columns. Apparently inspired by the ubiquitous lotus, the naturalistic plant forms terminate in a strange capital which might well not be recognized as a stylized lotus flower were it not that the top surface, above eye level and hence not visible to the average visitor, is carved with a representation of the inside of the open flower. Surging upwards with exuberant vitality, the surface of their sturdy, trunk-like forms animated with exquisite arabesques of tendril, frond and whorl, the columns irresistibly call to mind Bernini's twisted bronze columns of the *baldacchino* of St. Peter's (Fig. 7).

The Kiri or 'Milk' Dagoba is in an extremely fine state of preservation, with the original coat of white *chunam* still intact over considerable areas. Hence the name 'Milk Dagoba'. Although of comparatively modest scale, it is still more than twice the size of the Thuparama Dagoba at Anuradhapura, it has particularly fine proportions, and a most attractive patina, redolent of age without a hint of decrepitude. To my mind it is the most satisfying of all the dagobas of Ceylon. It shares a vast elevated podium with several structures, chief of them the *Lankatilaka* or 'Ornament of Lanka' (42) built, as the *Culavamsa* informs us, to house a colossal standing image of the Buddha so beautiful as to constitute 'an elixir for the eyes'. The largest temple in Ceylon, its 12 ft thick walls, 170 ft long by 80 ft wide, still rise to a height of 80 ft, though formerly they must have been well over 100 ft high. Within, at the end of the roofless nave, stands a brick Buddha image some 60 ft tall. Alas, the headless Buddha is no longer 'an elixir for the eyes' but a rather melancholy – if awe-inspiring sight. The great interest of the

55 Stairway up the step-pyramid Temple of Pre Rup, Angkor, Cambodia

56 Gilded votive Buddha image in the Shwezigon Pagoda, Pagan, Burma

Lankatilaka derives from its fusion of Buddhist and Hindu decorative elements and it is the Hindu elements of this building, whose other name is the Jetawanarama, the Temple said to have been erected by the Sage himself at Kapilavastu, that, ironically are its most fascinating feature. The great external wall surfaces are decorated with representations moulded in brick and finished in *chunam* of typical South-Indian structures (Plate 23). With their multi-tiered, many-turreted roofs, these vividly recall the *rathas* of Mamallapuram (43).

The mingling of Buddhist and Hindu concepts during the Polonnaruwa period extended far beyond stylistic plagiarism to the very deities worshipped at the shrines. Although subordinate to the Buddha, Vishnu was venerated as the 'Protector of Ceylon'.

Fig. 7 Spiral column of King Nissanka's 'Floral Altar', Polonnaruwa

Particularly popular was the worship of Pattini Devi as Goddess of Chastity and Controller of Epidemics, introduced to Ceylon at an early date. According to Sinhalese tradition – for there are many variations of the theme – Pattini's husband was wrongly accused by a goldsmith of the theft of the Queen of Madura's 'hollow, jingling, gem-set anklet' and was executed without a trial. In revenge, Pattini cursed the royal family and the city. From the day her husband had been beheaded, no rain fell in the kingdom and there was famine, fever and smallpox. Only when the worship of the chaste widow as a goddess was inaugurated, and one thousand goldsmiths sacrificed at her altar, did rain fall again and famine and pestilence disappear from the kingdom.

A traditional Sinhalese game recalling an incident in the life of the goddess is played in her honour. While Pattini and her husband were trying to break a flower off the top of a *sapu* tree with two hooked sticks, the hooks became interlocked and try as they may, they could not get them apart. Finally they called their friends to help them, the men joining the husband and the women Pattini, and in the tug-of-war the men's hook was broken at last amidst the jeers of the women.

The sacred *An Keliya* or 'Horns Game' takes place annually in some districts of Ceylon, in others only when famine or pestilence threatens. It commences with an elaborate purification ceremony at which the objects to be used in the ceremony are sprinkled with saffron water and covered with flowers, all to the accompaniment of drums, trumpets and cymbals, and the jingling of hollow anklets and bracelets such as caused the downfall of Pattini's husband. In one of the many local variations of the game, teams of villagers pull ropes attached to deer-horn. 'Membership of one or other team is hereditary; and so strong is the party feeling or jealousy between them that those of one side usually avoid marriage with the members of the families belonging to the other side' (44) – a situation which cannot but bring to mind the intense rivalry between the various *contrade* participating in the *Palio* of Siena. When, in the tug-of-war one horn finally snaps, the winning side taunts the losers with foul language and obscene gestures, intended to frighten away the evil spirits of pestilence and misfortune. Robert Knox, the seventeenth-century English merchant who was captured by the King of Kandy and spent 18 years in Ceylon before his escape, observed that 'Upon the breaking of the stick, that Party that hath won doth not a little rejoice, which rejoicing is exprest by Dancing and Singing, and uttering such sordid, beastly Expressions together with Postures of their Bodies, as I omit to write them, it being their shame in acting, and would be mine in rehearsing. For he is at that time most renowned that behaves himself most shameless and beastlike' (45).

It is difficult to associate such ribaldry – or, conversely, the concept of chastity – with the splendid, regal and sensuous image of the goddess in the British Museum

(Plate 5). This almost life-size image of pale bronze, originally gilt, has been in the Museum since 1830 and is one of the greatest treasures of its Oriental Department. Whether considered simply as a representation of feminine charm, as a symbol of the sap-like forces of fecundity welling within the taut yet supple flesh, or purely as an abstract composition of masses and volumes, it is one of the supreme masterpieces of Oriental Art. Its very uniqueness has made this image very difficult to date. Most certainly not later than the twelfth century, it may be much older as the rendering of the anatomy of hips and waist, as also that of the clinging drapery, is worthy of the best traditions of Gupta sculpture.

Mahayana Buddhist elements seem also to have thoroughly infiltrated the basic Theravada doctrine during the Polonnaruwa Period. Several deities of the Greater Vehicle appear on the temple façade, and among the bronzes from Ceylon now in the British Museum, is the most unusual Avalokitesvara Padmapani standing back to back with his *sakti* or female manifestation upon a lotus pedestal, 'emblematic of a deity representing the highest transcendental essence' (46), and holding an enormous lotus bud (Plate 24). We have here a Bodhisattva, a being who is entitled to Buddhahood and escape from the cycle of birth and rebirth through an accumulation of good deeds, but elects instead to defer this personal bliss in order to help others attain enlightenment – a saviour concept far removed, indeed, from the inexorable 'Wheel of Cause and Effect' of the Hinayana Doctrine (47).

In a particularly charming pastoral setting, a secluded clearing in the jungle where a few placid water-buffalo graze languidly on the cropped sward, lies the Gal Vihara (properly the *Kalu Gal Vihara* or 'Black Rock Shrine'). This is a rock-cut temple celebrated for its sculpture. The whole complex was fashioned at the command of the great Parakrama Bahu from one enormous granite outcrop. The dominant element of the composition is a truly gigantic, reclining Buddha in the act of entering *nirvana*, nearly fifty feet in length; stretched out full-length in the posture dictated by convention, he lies on his right side, head resting gently on his hand which is supported by a bolster, left arm extended along the top of the body. The figure is remarkable for its suggestion of relaxed repose, of deep sleep rather than death, singularly befitting to the voluntary 'self-extinction' of the Enlightened One.

Far more outstanding aesthetically is its companion piece, a standing figure of the disciple Ananda mourning the passing of his Master. Nearly 23 ft tall, the monumental figure is carved in such high relief as to appear completely free-standing from the front. The head is especially noteworthy (Plate 10). The expression of restrained yet absolute grief rivals Giotto's masterpieces in the Arena Chapel at Padua in its simplicity and power. The adjoining *vihara* proper is carved from the living rock in the manner of the cave-temples of India, two spurs of rock in the shape of columns being left on the exposed vertical face to support the enormous weight of stone overhead. In contrast to the stark simplicity of the Ananda figure, devoid of specific iconographic adjuncts, and thereby perhaps all the more universal in its appeal, the Buddha in the cave is seated upon a high lion-throne and framed by an elaborate aureole decorated with *devatas* at their devotions, lions rampant and attendants holding *chowries* or ceremonial fly-whisks (Plate 21).

On the opposite side of the cave from the recumbent Buddha and Ananda is another great seated Buddha executed in a singularly severe and grand style, completing a unique ensemble.

In complete contrast is the 'Lotus Bath' (Plate 16), one of the slightest monuments of Polonnaruwa, but one which seems a distillation of the beauty, elegance and refinement of this urbane civilization. The bath consists of five concentric rings of granite each scalloped to form a stylized, eight-petalled form, and diminishing in diameter as they descend, creating a step at each layer – as beautiful a solution as it is practical. The whole resembles nothing so much as a gigantic lotus in stone. Though its precise use is unknown, its feminine grace has prompted the title of 'Queen's Bath'.

A colossal sculpture eleven and a half feet tall, carved in high relief from a granulite outcrop at Polonnaruwa is traditionally supposed to be a portrait of Parakrama Bahu I (Plate 20). The remarkable individuality of both features and figure would seem to confirm that we are dealing with the representation of a specific person. The grandeur of this superb work derives from the success with which these portrait elements have been merged with more general concepts of dignity and age to form an unsurpassed archetype of the wise patriarch upholding the sacred traditions of his people.

The glory that was Polonnaruwa was destined to be short-lived. The years following the death of Parakrama Bahu in 1186 witnessed a fall so rapid and complete that, like the chronicler of the *Culavamsa* one is tempted to attribute it to divine wrath. Except for the reign of the usurper, Nissanka Malla, there was an almost continuous round of internecine strife. Four successive monarchs were murdered, one after a reign of five days; the fifth was deposed by the widow of the great Parakrama Bahu, who in turn was deposed, restored and again deposed. On to this scene of near-anarchy stepped the Tamil chieftain Magha, smarting for revenge. In 1214 A.D. he invaded with a force of twenty thousand warriors. 'And like a scorching fire burning down the forest of the good, he conquered the land of Lanka – And his warriors stripped the people of their garments and ornaments and cut off the hands and feet of captives. They put fetters on the wealthy, tortured them and left them beggars; wrecked the image houses, ravaged the monasteries, tormented the comrades of the Five Orders (48) and made of the people beasts of burden. Wantonly, they tore the famous books from their cords and strewed the leaves hither and thither. Even the great and lofty *dagobas*, like the Ruanweli, embodying the glory of former pious kings, did not escape. They too were overthrown and, alas! alas! many of the sacred relics – the very souls of the monuments, as it were – were lost. They captured the great capital of Polonnaruwa and the king – and they put out the monarch's eyes and plundered all his treasures, pearls and jewels. Even so did the Tamils, like the giants of Mara, destroy the kingdom and the land.'

This time there was no renaissance. The ensuing centuries saw a continuous retreat towards the refuge of the central mountains, with the Sinhalese capital successively at a dozen different sites. At Kandy in the central highlands they maintained a limited state and dominion, while the Tamil Kingdoms of Jaffna ruled in the north and the lowlands and coastal area fell successively to the Portuguese, Dutch and British, who, in 1815 deposed the last King of Kandy and established their sovereignty over the whole island.

Meanwhile the charred ruins of Polonnaruwa stood deserted, and were slowly but relentlessly submerged beneath the engulfing tide of the jungle; the life-giving 'tanks', breached and neglected, changed to miasmic swamps infested by the malarial mosquito, and the northern plain, scene of Lanka's glory, which through man's ingenuity had been made to blossom like the rose, returned to its primordial state: an uninhabited drought-stricken forest.

2 Pagan

The City of a Myriad Pagodas

The earliest inhabitants of Burma of whom we have any knowledge were the Mons and the Pyus. The Mons, closely related to the Mon-Khmers of Cambodia, probably immigrated from South China at a very early date – at any rate before making contact with Chinese culture. The Pyus arrived later from their original home in Eastern Tibet. Already in the early centuries of our era we find a Mon kingdom in Lower Burma with its capital at Thaton – later to be split into two, with a rival capital at Pegu – and the Pyu established in Central Burma with their capital at Srikshetra (Sanskrit: The City of Splendour) (49).

Contact with India had been established at a very early date, possibly as early as the third century B.C. during the reign of the Emperor Asoka. Both Chinese sources and the Pali chronicles confirm the presence of Indian merchants and savants in Burma in the opening centuries of our era.

The closeness of these contacts, and the fact that the Burmese name for the Mons is *Talaing*, supposedly after the Dravidian Telinga people, has led some scholars (50) to suppose that the Mon people as a whole, and not merely an Indianized elite, came originally from the east coast of India. 'The cultural aspects of Mon society and that represented by Pyu Srikshetra were in many respects similar. Gupta cultural influence was much in evidence in both of them. The ashes of the dead were buried in urns, the costliness of the containers corresponding with the social status of the deceased. Both peoples were interested in trade, the Mons as a maritime people in their own right and the Pyus as controllers of the Irrawaddy River artery which constituted the southern end of the overland trading route from Western China.' (51)

A Chinese chronicle of the T'ang Dynasty paints a vivid picture of life at a Pyu capital – probably Srikshetra – around 800 A.D. 'The city wall, faced with green-glazed brick is 160 *li* in circumference and has twelve gates and pagodas at each of the four corners. Within, there are more than a hundred monasteries, all resplendent with gold, silver and cinnabar. Likewise the palace of the sovereign. The women wear their hair in a top-knot ornamented with flowers, pearls and precious stones – and are trained in music and the dance. Having no oil, they use candles of perfumed bees-wax. The people have a knowledge of astronomy and delight in the Law of the Buddha. At the age of seven, both boys and girls shave their heads and go to live at a monastery as novices until they are twenty. If at this age they have not awakened to the religious life, they once again allow their hair to grow and return to the town. The people deplore the taking of life. Their clothing is of cotton, for they maintain that silk should not be worn as it involves injury to the silkworm.'

In the eighth century the Mons of Pegu conquered the Pyu capital of Srikshetra and established a new northern capital at Old Pagan. Shortly after, there was a new influx of semi-nomadic, Tibeto-Burman peoples, probably moving south to escape conscription under the tyrannical regime of Nanchao in present-day

57 Ava Period frescoes; Apsaras on the vault of the Upali Thein, Pagan, Burma

58 Ava Period frescoes; scene of Burmese town life in the Ananda Monastery, Pagan, Burma

57

58

Yunnan. These were the ancestors of the Burmese proper. Distant relatives of the Pyus, they were, by the testimony of their own historians, still in a primitive stage of civilization. They had no culture or letters to speak of, but they were skilled in the arts of war and horsemanship and had acquired the art of rice cultivation and terracing. Spreading out over Central Burma, they absorbed the surviving remnants of the recently-defeated Pyus – a process probably greatly facilitated by their racial affinity – and eventually founded their capital at Pagan, strategically situated on a bank of the Irrawaddy River near the confluence with its chief tributary, the Chindwin.

The original faith of the Burmese was a primitive animism, centred around the worship of the Thirty Six *Nats* (from the Pali, *natha:* a Lord). These were of two categories: native spirits of the sky, trees, water and other natural phenomena, and the wraiths of heroes and ancestors who had met a violent death. Propitiation of these spirits was essential to ensure prosperity and good fortune, for if neglected, even the most benign was apt to become vindictive and hostile. The two most celebrated were a brother and sister pair, the *Mahagiri Nats*, believed to reside on Mount Popa, a hill near Pagan. Their annual festival was a drunken orgy at which frenzied spirit-mediums pronounced their oracles – as celebrated in the palmy days of Pagan as those of Delphi and Olympus.

At the time of the arrival of the Burmese, Lower Burma had already been converted to the Hinayana Doctrine of Buddhism for many centuries. The celebrated missionary-commentator Buddhaghosa is credited with personally bringing the sacred books of the Pali canon to Thaton around 450 A.D. Brahmanism also played a minor role, as is attested to by Vishnuite rites and traces of Sivaite phallic worship. As was customary in all the 'Indianized' cultures, even Buddhist rulers retained learned Brahmins as advisors, at least on secular matters. There is also evidence of Mahayana Buddhism which, however, did not ever appear to have presented a serious challenge to the Hinayana form.

In Upper Burma the position seems to have been reversed. Here, due probably to its connections with Manipur and Nepal, the Mahayana Doctrine generally prevailed. A debased sect of Tibetan Buddhism, practised by heretical priests known as the *Ari* assumed great importance at Pagan. The habits of the *Ari* were anything but what one associates with the gentle monks of the Hinayana Doctrine: They wore their hair long, drank hard-liquor, rode horseback into battle, summoned spirits from the dead, and practised alchemy. They also indulged in Tantric sex-orgies. These symbolized the union of the Buddha and his *Sakti* (or female principle); Siva and his consort, the positive and negative forces of the universe, priest and female initiate 'attaining together to a realization of the immanence within themselves of the consubstantiality of the God and Goddess' (52). During the reign of Nyaung-U (931-964) the cult of the *Ari* became virtually the official religion of Pagan.

The Burmese at this stage seem to have made remarkably little progress since their arrival, especially when one takes into account their close contact for almost two centuries with the thousand-year-old cultures of the Mon and Pyu. Constant internal dissensions were perhaps the reason. But within the next few years there was to be a dramatic change which would transform Pagan from a provincial back-water into a great centre of learning and culture and one of the architectural marvels of the East.

59 Guardian Ape, Temple of Banteay Srei, Angkor, Cambodia

King Anawrahta was the son of a usurper who had seized the throne from Nyaung-U but had in turn been forced to retire to a monastery by Nyaung-U's sons.

In 1044 Anawrahta slew the surviving son in single combat and became king.

According to The Glass Palace Chronicle (53), Anawrahta, 'being a king of ripe perfections . . . was displeased by the lawless doings of the *Ari*, knowing them for false doctrine . . . And he yearned vehemently to discover The True Law.'

A young monk from Thaton named Shin Arahan journeyed north to Pagan, where he lived as a hermit outside the walls of the city. Although a Brahmin by descent, he had been schooled in the Orthodox Theravada Doctrine of Hinayana Buddhism. Shin Arahan was brought to the attention of Anawrahta who 'was glad like the young bud of a lotus that has found sunshine', for the monk's noble bearing made him feel sure that the True Law would be found within him. The king requested Shin Arahan to stay on in Pagan and expound the Theravada Doctrine. To do so, explained Shin Arahan, he would require scriptures, 'for without the scriptures there can be no study and without study there can be no intuition'. He suggested that Anawrahta ask King Manuha of Thaton for the loan of one of his thirty complete copies of the *Tripitakas* (54) written in the Pali language. So Anawrahta sent a minister bearing rich gifts to the Mon ruler. His courteous request for the scriptures was, however, brusquely refused. Furious at the insult, Anawrahta assembled an army and swept down on Thaton. And he 'captured King Manuha . . . with his family and ministers . . . and he brought away the sacred relics which were kept in a jewelled casket and worshipped by a line of kings in Thaton; and he placed the thirty sets of the Pitakas on the king's thirty-two white elephants . . . and he brought away such men as were skilled in carving, turning, and painting; masons, moulders of plaster and flower-patterns; blacksmiths, silversmiths, braziers, founders of gongs and cymbals, filagree flower-workers; doctors, and trainers of elephants and horses; makers of shields, forgers of cannon, muskets and bows; men skilled in frying, parching, baking and frizzling; *Yakin* hairdressers, and men cunning in perfumes, odours, and the juices of flowers. Moreover, to the noble Order acquainted with the books of the Pitakas he made fair appeal and brought them away.'

Flushed with the success of his campaign against Thaton, Anawratha also ravaged the ancient Pyu capital of Old Prome and firmly established Burmese hegemony.

The conquest of Thaton in 1056 ushered in the Golden Age of Pagan. The presence of the captive scholars, priests and artisans, and of a labour force of some thirty thousand, acted as a catalyst on the robust but relatively rude culture of the Burmese. The Mon alphabet was adopted and a period of extraordinary architectural and artistic activity began.

The captive King Manuha was treated with respect by Anawrahta and even permitted to hold a subsidiary court. Several buildings at Pagan were dedicated by him, among them the Nanpaya Temple which he is said to have financed by the sale of his great jewelled ring.

The architectural remains at Pagan fall into two main categories. Firstly, the stupas (55) here, as in Ceylon, solid masses of masonry protecting a sealed chamber containing relics. The stupas of Pagan are so numerous and of such variety of contour as to constitute a veritable architectural text-book, reflecting influences from as far afield as India, Ceylon, Indonesia, Cambodia and Tibet. Secondly, there are the temples whose main function is to house sacred images and provide space for the devotions associated with these images.

The use of the true radiating arch – and not the corbelled arch of India – to bridge these spaces with vaults is most surprising (Plate 27). Although familiar

60 Brick and stucco tower-shrine at the Bakong, 'Roluos Group', Angkor, Cambodia

61 Female deity; Temple of Banteay Srei, Angkor, Cambodia

61

62

with the true arch, the Indians very seldom use it, disliking its dynamism or, as they expressed it, the fact that the arch 'never sleeps'.

Many theories have been offered as to why the builders of Pagan, otherwise so respectful of Indian precept, should have flaunted it in this respect. The derivation of the arch from some other source than India – Central Asia or the Muslim world, for example – has been suggested. Griswold propounds a most appealing theory: that the extremely heavy masses of masonry at Pagan, in which openings are always very small in relation to the solid mass, provide the key to the evasion of the Indian interdict. In such situations, thrusts can safely be ignored and 'nothing about the vaults need shock Indian sentiment if they are thought of – as indeed they must be – not as a means of roofing a space, but as a means of reinforcing a cave (56). Be this as it may, there is no doubt that the preservation of Pagan's monuments owes much to the stability of the true arch. Brick was the chief building material used. Although mud- rather than lime-mortar was favoured, the jointing was unusually fine, so that the strength was not seriously impaired and masses of load-bearing masonry 200 ft in height were feasible. Stone was occasionally employed for trim and the fabric protected from the effects of the weather by a coating of stucco. Where the original coating still remains intact – as it does over surprisingly large areas – it is noteworthy for its exquisite decoration (Plates 42 and 43).

Fig. 8 One of the 37 *Nats* enshrined in the pavilion of the Shwezigon Pagoda, Pagan

The most important monument dating from Anawrahta's reign is the Shwezigon Pagoda, built to house the most sacred of Pagan's newly-acquired relics: the frontal bone and a tooth of the Buddha.

In the Glass Palace Chronicle we read that the tooth relic was encased in a jewelled casket and placed on the back of a sacred white elephant. The animal was then let loose and the pagoda erected on the divinely-appointed spot where the elephant came to rest – this despite the fact that the site so chosen was on shifting sand necessitating elaborate foundations.

It may be noted in passing that the reason for the particular veneration accorded 'white elephants' – in reality an albino of the species – is that the Buddha, during the last of his prior existences as a Bodhisattva, is said to have assumed this form. Among the Burmese and Thai a white elephant is looked upon as a royal treasure beyond compare, and an augur of good fortune and prosperity (57).

The Shwezigon Pagoda is a pyramidal mass comprising a series of terraces, the lower square, the upper round, elaborated with gateways, stairs, and miniature spires, and surmounted by a virile, bell-shaped, *stupa* spire. Though apparently based on a Pyu prototype, judged from remains at Shrikshetra, this bell-shape may rightly be regarded as typically Burmese and has served as the model for innumerable pagodas throughout the country.

Anawrahta did everything in his power to make his great pagoda the focal point of religious ardour at Pagan. He even placed images of the Nats (Fig. 8) in a subsidiary structure within the sacred precincts, the original pantheon of 36 *Nats* being augmented by a 37th member: The Buddha himself. To criticism of this act, Anawrahta replied 'Men will not come for the sake of the new faith. Let them come for their old gods and gradually they will be won over.' The tolerant syncreticism of Buddhism could hardly be better exemplified.

62 Male deity; Temple of Banteay Srei, Angkor, Cambodia

63 Baksei Chamron Temple, Angkor, Cambodia

Thanks to the exceptional sanctity of its relics and its close association with her hero-warrior-founder-king, the Shwezigon has become something of a national shrine to the Burmese. Its golden *hti* or umbrella, crowning the monument, is encrusted with precious jewels and the whole edifice has recently been regilded with pure gold-leaf (Plate 33).

Anawrahta was gored to death by a wild buffalo in 1077 and after a brief reign his ineffectual elder son and successor was deposed by his brother, Kyanzittha, one of the greatest rulers of Pagan. This valiant and statesmanlike king sought to consolidate his dominion by persuasion rather than force. To this end he gave his daughter in marriage to the heir of the Thaton Mons, a descendant of King Manuha, and decreed that their son, and not his own, would succeed to the throne.

Mon culture thoroughly permeated the fabric of Burmese culture during the reign of Kyanzittha. The redoubtable Primate, Shin Arahan, continued to wield great power as the close confidant of the king, and Mon scholars and administrators occupied important positions. Kyanzittha himself seems to have had a particular fondness for all things Mon: the Mon language was used exclusively for inscriptions and the Mon style triumphed in building and the arts. Indeed, the chief monument of Kyanzittha's reign, the magnificent and venerable Ananda Temple, may with good reason be regarded as the culminating masterpiece of Mon architecture.

The Ananda Temple was founded in 1091 A.D. and is one of the very few temples to have remained continuously in use since its consecration, through all the city's subsequent vicissitudes. The name, Ananda, is generally supposed to be derived from *Ananta Panna* (Endless Wisdom) (58). The corruption of the name was probably due to the familiarity of the people with Ananda, disciple of Buddha. Large gateways at the four cardinal points afford access to the spacious walled court in which the temple stands. In essence, the main structure is a cube, some 175 ft square and 35 ft high, expressed on the façade as two superimposed tiers of windows defined by pilasters and a string course. A large gabled portico or vestibule some 57 ft long projects from the centre of each side of the square, the resultant form being a Greek cross of perfect symmetry with arms nearly 300 ft long. Over the main square mass rise two sloping roofs, and above the roofs, four narrow, receding terraces. The topmost terrace serves as the base for the tall gilded spire rising to 180 ft (Plate 44). This has the typical Burmese combination of *sikhara* (a mitre-like pyramid with bulging sides, adopted from the temples of India) and elongated bell-shaped dome, surmounted by a tapering, ringed finial, terminating in a gilded metal *hti*. Miniature versions of the spire accent the corners of the roofs and lowest terrace, enhancing the scale of the main *sikhara* by contrast, and lending variety to the silhouette, while large projecting dormer windows repeat the gabled form of the entrance porches below. The total effect is noteworthy for its soaring elegance, and the masterly ease with which a multitude of exuberant details have been co-ordinated into a compact unified mass. Within, two continuous, concentric corridors roofed by lofty ogee vaults provide for the ritual circumambulation.

The four entrances lead directly to the sanctum proper, an enormous cube of solid masonry supporting the central tower (Fig. 10). Each side of the cube contains a deep, high niche for the chief votive images: four colossal sculptures of the historic Buddhas of our eon who have already entered *nirvana*. Standing back to back against the central core, the 'Enlightened Ones', their faces suffused by an enigmatic half-smile, radiate beneficence towards the four cardinal points (Plates 29 and 35). The images tower forty feet above the worshippers and are lit through narrow lancet openings in the dormer windows high above, invisible from below. These permit a beam of light to penetrate to the heart of the temple-mountain and bathe the gilded images in a mysterious aureole of light – a *tour de force* unrivalled even by that prodigy of illusionistic lighting, the 'Trasparente' of Toledo Cathedral.

The inspiration for the Ananda Temple is traditionally held to have come

64 Head of the Buddha from Ta Prohm, Angkor, Cambodia. *Musée Guimet, Paris*

65 Sculptured pediment from the Temple of Banteay Srei: the demons Sounda and Aupasounda dispute possession of the Apsaras Tilottama. *Musée Guimet, Paris*

64

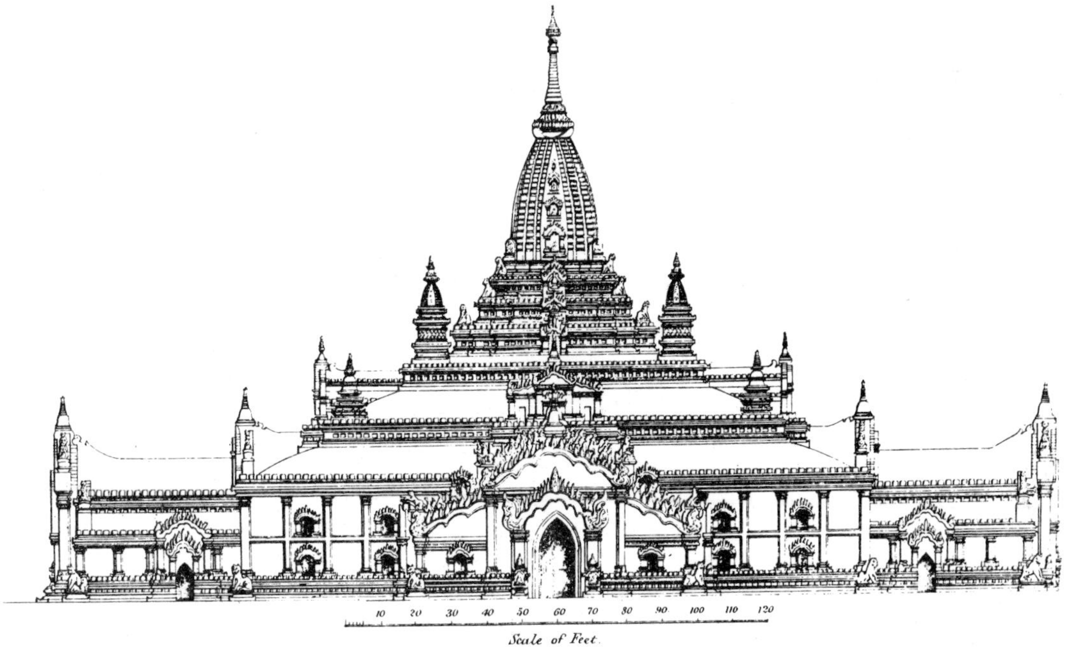

Fig. 9 Elevation of the Ananda Temple, from *A Narrative of the Mission sent by the Governor-General of India to the Court of Ava*, by Sir Henry Yule, 1858

directly from India. The Glass Palace Chronicle relates that King Kyanzittha was struck by the noble deportment of eight strange Buddhist monks who stood before the palace for alms. In answer to his enquiry, the monks told him they came from India where they had dwelt in a celebrated cave-temple on the Nandamula Mountain in the Himalayas. This they described to the king who was so impressed that he conceived the idea of building a great temple which would reproduce the main features of the cave-temple.

The fact that the design of the Ananda Temple displays many Mon characteristics (59), does not of itself discount the legend, for even the most original concept would doubtless be executed in the currently prevailing style. Nor, again, does the fact that the monks more likely came from the region of Orissa; for their cave-monastery there might well have been a symbolic representation of sacred Mount Meru in the Himalayas, which would merely have reached Burma at one further remove. Certainly, the final effect could hardly be more appropriate to the purported symbolism. The dark interior is far more suggestive of a void hollowed out of a solid mass than of constructed space (60). Especially when seen from a distance across the parched plain, the enormous white bulk of the temple, rising in serried tiers, resembles a snow-clad mountain range, and the gleaming spire a solitary peak, caught in the last rays of the sun.

It is difficult for the Westerner with his rational approach to architecture to make a just assessment of the 'functional' qualities of Indian – or Indian-inspired – religious architecture. In the case of the Hindu and Buddhist temple it must always be borne in mind that the *raison d'etre* of the structure is not so much a meeting-place for the faithful as the dwelling-place of a god, represented by his image. To be effective, and, therefore, 'functional' in the strict etymological sense, the earthly dwelling should be an acceptable earthly counterpart of the deity's celestial abode: sacred Mount Meru. The yardstick is thus whether or not this

66 Stucco decoration at Preah Ko, 'Roluos Group', Angkor, Cambodia

cosmological symbolism has been effectively expressed, rather than whether practical problems have been solved in the most rational manner. There can be no doubt that the Ananda fulfils its design criteria most admirably.

Inserted in niches along the outer corridor of the Ananda Temple, their cinnabar and gilt finish particularly telling in the subdued light, is a series of eighty-one stone reliefs narrating the principal events in the life of Gautama Buddha (Plates 36, 37 and 40). Of inspired simplicity, animation and grace, they display a remarkable inventiveness in the handling of conventional themes and represent the high-water mark of Burmese classical sculpture.

When the time of her confinement drew near, Queen Mahadevi, the mother of the Buddha, felt an irrepressible desire to visit her parents. She requested permission of her husband, who straightway had the route from Kapilavastu to Devadaha beautifully decorated and sent his queen to her parents. In the Ananda Temple relief (Plate 36), Queen Mahadevi, of imposing size as befits her station, is depicted on her litter borne by sixteen attendants – only the eight on the near side being visible. Behind, yet another attendant holds the royal umbrella over her head.

The legend of the ascetic Kaladevala is the subject of Plate 37. Now in the Trayastrimsa Paradise the heavenly beings rejoiced and sported, waving their turbans and saying: 'In the city of Kapilavastu a son has been born to King Suddhodana. One day, sitting upon the Throne of Wisdom, he will become a Buddha.' The ascetic Kaladevala through his supernatural powers repaired to the Trayastrimsa Paradise and was not a little astonished to find the gods delirious with joy. Having learnt the reason, he went straightway to Kapilavastu and asked the king to show him the child. And King Suddhodana ordered the child to be brought, took him and held him towards the hermit so that he might salute the holy man: But the child, 'than whom none was greater', turned up his feet and placed them on the ascetic's head. Kaladevala understood, rose from his seat and saluted the future Buddha by bringing his joined hands to his forehead; and the king, seeing this marvel, himself did reverence to his son. It was then that the hermit predicted that the child would become a Buddha.

To the art lover, Kyanzittha's name is linked first and foremost with the Ananda Temple, but to the Burmese his greatest claim to fame is that he restored the great Buddhist temple at Bodhgaya in India. This, the most sacred shrine of Buddhism, erected on the site of 'The Great Enlightenment', had fallen into sad disrepair with the decay of Buddhism in India. Kyanzittha's act of piety must have enormously increased the prestige of the Burmese kingdom. It is recorded in inscriptions at Bodhgaya and recalled by a replica of the famous shrine, The Mahabodhi Temple, erected in Pagan a century later. Though poor in detail, its *sikhara* preserves the powerful shape of the Bodhgaya original. Seen against a blue sky, its white mass is extremely picturesque (Plate 31).

Pagan at this period was becoming increasingly celebrated as a centre of Buddhist learning, the process doubtless being greatly accelerated by the arrival of refugee-scholars from India, many from the famous Buddhist university and missionary training-centre of Nalanda in Bihar. There, Buddhism was already declining rapidly and was to be dealt a death-blow when the Muslim invasion swept down the Ganges valley in the twelfth century, sacking the great monasteries which were the remaining stronghold of the Buddhist faith.

The interior of the typical, Mon-style temple is very dark. Not only are the window openings small, but the light penetration is further filtered down by the use of perforated stone screens. This is well illustrated by a window from the

67 Bird-headed guardian deity, Temple of Banteay Srei, Angkor, Cambodia

68 Bas-relief on the north 'library' at Banteay Srei: Indra, the Thunder God, sends down beneficent rains on a rejoicing animal and plant kingdom, Angkor, Cambodia

69 Spiral gable terminal. Temple of Banteay Srei, Angkor, Cambodia

66

67

68

69

71

Kubyaukkyi Temple at Myinpagan, erected by Rajakumar, a son of Kyanzittha (Plate 34). The liveliness of the well-proportioned pattern of perforations and the richness of the delicate stucco decoration of pilasters and triangular pediment, are outstanding. Offset by the plain stucco wall which provides just the required measure of restraint, the ensemble is probably the finest of its kind at Pagan.

The cornice frieze above, detailed in (Plate 42), employs a decorative element so popular as to become virtually a *leitmotiv* at Pagan: ogres discharging chaplets of pearls – or are they merely garlands of plucked blooms threaded on a string, such as are still commonly offered at the temples by the devout?

Rajakumar was an illegitimate son of Kyanzittha and is remembered chiefly as the author of the Myazedi Stele. This, through its parallel inscriptions in Pali, Mon, Pyu, is of great epigraphic and historic importance and served as Burma's 'Rosetta Stone'.

Kyanzittha was succeeded by his grandson, Alaungsithu, a scholar perfectly at home in the Pali language, if we are to judge from an inscription in fine verse attributed to him. He was also an ardent temple-builder. His reign marks the end of Mon cultural dominance and the emergence of a truly Burmese style. The key monument of this transitional phase is the Thatbyinnyu Temple built in 1144 A.D.

The strict symmetry of the Ananda Temple with its four central images has been abandoned for a single, great seated Buddha facing east. Only the eastern portico projects from the main mass. Whereas Mon-style temples rarely have more than one storey, the Thatbyinnyu has no fewer than four. The two lowest served as cells for the monks, the third and main floor houses the chief cult image, raised high within the building mass, the fourth floor housed the library, and above this is a pagoda enshrining relics, so that the building is, strictly speaking, a combination of *stupa* and temple. Externally the roofs are flat, a practical expedient providing usable terraces, but far less effective visually than the sweeping continuity afforded by the sloping roofs of the Ananda Temple. The gilded metal *hti* rises to a height of 201 ft overlooking all the other monuments of Pagan (Fig. 10).

The accession of Narapatisithu in 1174 marked the end of Mon influence at court. Whether precipitated by political considerations we are not sure, but after this date all royal inscriptions were couched in Burmese – simple and vigorous if lacking in the poetic quality of the Mon.

Relations with Ceylon which had reached a nadir during the preceding interregnum, due to bitter trade rivalry, were restored and the Theravada school of Hinayana Buddhism was introduced anew from the Island Kingdom. Differing chiefly on points of monastic discipline the Sinhalese branch soon became dominant as the 'Latter Order', to distinguish it from the Mon or 'Former Order'.

Narapatisithu's reign saw the final triumph of the Burmese style in architecture in such monuments as the Sulamani Temple (Plate 32). The supreme masterpiece of the style is the Gawdawpalin or 'Throne of the Ancestral Hall', commemorating the practice of paying homage to the *manes* of the royal ancestors (Plate 38). Smaller in area and far less complicated in plan and detailing than either the Ananda or the Thatbyinnyu, it is, nevertheless, about the same height. Though some of the decorative detail has suffered much through barbarously inept restoration, the general effect is extremely fine due to the excellent proportions.

The awkward function between the two main vertical elements of the Thatbyinnyu has here been perfectly resolved, bridged by the insistent verticals of large-scale flamboyant gable ends and miniature stupas which leap skyward in a paean of exaltation. Gone are the dark interiors of the Mon period, so charged

70 Head of a Bodhisattva. *Musée Guimet, Paris*

71 Bronze statuette of a dancing Apsaras in the style of the Bayon. *Museum of Fine Arts, Boston*

with drama and mystery. If they evoked the atmosphere of a Romanesque crypt, the ample light now admitted through far larger openings, and playing on surfaces of whitewash and gilt, suggested rather the light-hearted character of some South-German rococo church.

A characteristic of the temples of the late Pagan period is the extremely architectonic quality of the massing which lends them a universal, almost inevitable air. Perhaps it is this that, despite the exotic elements, gives rise to a curious sensation of familiarity on the part of European beholders. This was already remarked upon by the orientalist, Sir Henry Yule, who, as a young officer with the British Army in Burma in the middle of the nineteenth century, was the first European visitor to appreciate the importance of Pagan. He later made a careful study of the main monuments, including measured drawings which are still today the standard references (Figs. 9, 10, 11). Of the Gawdawpalin he writes: 'Gleaming in its white plaster, with numerous pinnacles and tall central spire, we had seen it from far down the Irrawaddy rising like a dim version of Milan Cathedral'; and of the great temples in general: 'They all suggest strange memories of the temples of Southern Catholic Europe' (61).

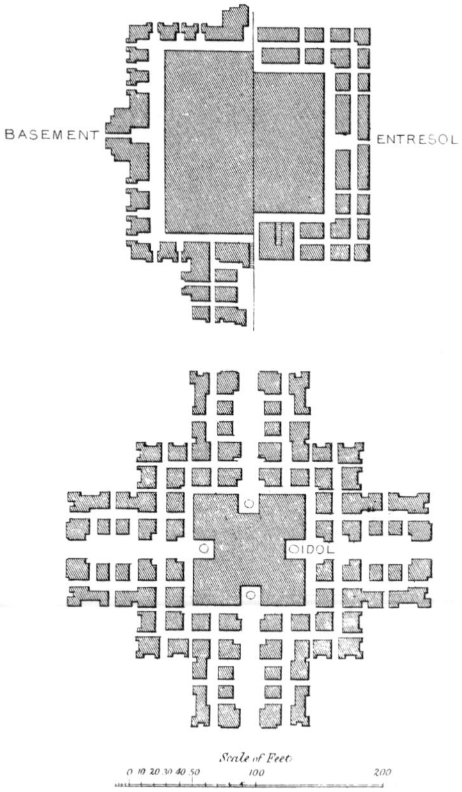

Fig. 10 Plans of the Thatbyinnyu (*above*) and Ananda (*below*) Temples, from . . . *Mission* . . . *to the Court of Ava*, by Sir Henry Yule, 1858

A wishful missionary went so far astray by the resemblance as earnestly to inquire 'Can these buildings not have owed their origin to the skill of a Western Christian or Missionary, who may have adopted largely the ornamentation of the Burmese, and ingrafted much of their detail and arrangements on his own idea of a temple? May not the true cross-like plan of the Ananda be thus symbolical, and may he not have looked forward to the time when this noble pile might be turned from the worship of an unknown god to the service of the Most High?'

Scenes from the 'Great Life' of the Buddha, such as those portrayed on the bas-reliefs of the Ananda Temple, are always imbued with the appropriate hieratic solemnity. Forming a prelude, as it were, to the historic life of the Buddha, are the 550 *jataka* tales which relate those previous existences during which he stored up a sufficient body of virtue to entitle him to Buddhahood in his final incarnation. Compounded of allegory and folk-tale, these *jatakas* imposed fewer conventions on the artist who was relatively free to depict them as he saw fit.

Among the chief attractions of Pagan are the numerous contemporary *jataka* cycles in fresco, terra-cotta and glazed ceramic (Plates 45, 46 and 47). Executed in a most spontaneous and humorous vein, they depict the Buddha as king, sage and merchant, and occasionally in such unlikely roles as a bird, she-tiger, monkey or sprite.

The touching naïveté of the execution of the plaque illustrated in Plate 47 accords perfectly with its theme: While a fowler lies asleep, his snares and newly-caught birds by his side, his decoy partridge inquires of a holy man whether its occupation is sinful and is assured that 'the absence of evil intention while in a state of coercion absolves it from all guilt'.

Although Mahayana doctrines never again posed a serious threat to the supremacy of the Hinayana school after the time of Anawrahta, they did not vanish completely. As in the case of animistic and Vishnuite cults, appealing features were incorporated within the overall Theravada framework. The *Ari* themselves reappeared later in the guise of astrologers, hawkers of amulets and phylacteries, and physicians; and with the triumph of a truly Burmese culture, there seems to have been a minor revival of the Mahayana School.

Several temples contain frescoes of Mahayana inspiration, often with strong Tantric overtones. Stylistically they reflect the influence of Bengal and Nepal.

Fig. 11 Elevation of the Thatbyinnyu Temple, from . . . *Mission . . . to the Court of Ava*, by Sir Henry Yule, 1858

Among the finest is the thirteenth-century fresco in the Nandamannya Temple depicting Avalokitesvara Padmapani (Plate 49). As befits a heavenly being who has progressed beyond the stage of differentiation of the sexes, the Androgynous figure exhibits a fusion of male form and female grace; while the subtle smile captures perfectly that combination of compassion and detachment personified by the merciful Bodhisattva.

The Dhammayazika Pagoda (Plate 39), symbolizing the Buddha as *Dhammaraja*, Ruler of Justice and Righteousness, was built by King Narapatisithu in 1197 A.D. The bell-shaped, stupa spire follows the classic precedent of the Shwezigon Pagoda, but the substructure is most unusual and elaborate. The lower circumambulatory terraces are pentagonal, and at the base on each side there is a small temple enshrining a Buddha image. This whole complex is raised on a platform enclosed by a wall, and this, in turn, enclosed by an outer circuit wall pierced by five gateways.

Such *stupas* as the Dhammayazika and the Mingalazedi represent a stage of classical perfection in the evolution of the massive early Indian and Sinhalese moulds into vertical, aspiring forms, later to dissolve into the soaring insubstantiality of the Shwe Dagon at Rangoon and the Thai pagodas. We have here a testimony in stone to a change in spiritual ideals and psychology analogous to that which distinguishes the Gothic from the Romanesque.

From a stone inscription in one of the five small temples around the base of the Dhammayazika Pagoda, we learn that Narapatisithu disbursed 44,027 *ticals* of silver as wages for the workmen and gave 18 *pes* (nearly 36 acres) of land. On the completion of the pagoda, the king further dedicated 1000 slaves, 500 of whom were Burman and 500 Indian, 500 *pes* of land and 500 bullocks for its maintenance.

'A large proportion of the slave population in Burma was apparently assigned to religious institutions. Persons so assigned, whether caretakers, cowherds, cooks, craftsmen, or musicians, kept their traditional vocational status. They frequently lived in their own separate villages, whose productive output belonged to the monastery. In fact the many listings of donations of pagoda slaves appearing in the inscriptions afford a cross-sectional view of Burman society. The craftsmen, for example, included masons and stone cutters, spinners and weavers, furniture and image makers, wood carvers, painters and decorators, blacksmiths and goldsmiths, and makers of pots, jugs and trays. Vocational groups included midwives, launderers, water carriers and canal diggers, boatmen, cartmen and harness makers, salt makers, barbers, manicurists, locksmiths, and armourers. The fact that slave status was acquired by large groups of debtors, captured rebels, and war prisoners and even by its voluntary acceptance, and the practice of keeping slaves together as functioning social units, suggest that life as a monastery slave carried no serious stigma and was perhaps superior in some respects to alternatives available for free members of the population. An estimated 10 per cent of Burma's slave population was literate. In any case, slavery was mildly imposed at Pagan; manumission could be purchased for the moderate sum of 5 vis of copper.' (62)

The enormous sums spent on religious foundations and their maintenance, coupled with the ever-increasing extent of church lands, exempt from taxation, were bound, eventually, to have a debilitating effect on the economy.

During the reign of Narapatisithu's successor, Nandaungmya (1210-1234), the last great ruler of Pagan, this problem was greatly aggravated by the rise of a new heretical sect, the *Arana*. These forest-dwelling monks, many of whose habits recall those of the *Ari*, adopted an aggressive policy of land annexation which they celebrated with riotous feasts at which great quantities of meat and alcohol were consumed.

A new Ordination Hall, the Upali Thein, was erected during the second quarter of the thirteenth century, as a sign of royal support for Orthodoxy. The interior of the Upali Thein contains a polychrome Buddha image on a high pedestal and is noteworthy for its exceptionally fine and well-preserved frescoes of the Ava Period (Back Jacket and Plate 57).

The Mingalazedi Stupa was consecrated by King Narathihapati in the year 1274. '. . . And inside were placed images of the twenty-eight Buddhas of the Seven Postures, and of the chief disciples, all cast in pure gold, and set with the Nine Jewels; and seated effigies of the fifty-one kings of Pagan and their wives, in pure silver . . . a cubit tall . . .' The relics of the Lord Buddha were encased in a gem-studded casket and placed on a richly-caparisoned, sacred, white she-elephant. And the route from the palace to the stupa was decorated with silken hangings and flowers . . . and the relics were transported in solemn procession, followed by the royal family and the princes of the blood, and the ministers, eight hundred in all, wearing ruby earrings and diadems, studded with pearls . . . And the king caused his daughters and the daughters of the

72 Sculptured stone door-jamb and pilaster, the Baphuon, Angkor, Cambodia

73 The great causeway and Temple of Angkor Wat, at sunset

ministers, also eight hundred in number, to do their hair in the *suli* knot and to wear apparel gorgeous with ornaments of rubies, emeralds and pearls . . . And after the relics of the Lord Buddha had been enshrined in the stupa, the king caused his family and ministers, the princesses and the daughters of the ministers to unstring and sever all their ornaments and offer them to the sacred relic chamber.'

This recital of regal pomp and splendour gives no inkling that the days of Pagan were already numbered.

The construction of the pagoda had, in fact, been dogged by a mysterious and ominous prophecy: 'The pagoda finished, the great country ruined.' When the soothsayers and the masters of magic interpreted this as meaning: 'When the Mingalazedi Pagoda is completed, the Kingdom of Pagan will be shattered to dust', the king abandoned the work for six full years.

Only the continual strictures of the Primate, enforced by learned disquisitions on the illusory nature of permanence and the warning that Narathihapati would undoubtedly be held up to scorn by future generations if he neglected to complete his good work, finally convinced the king to complete the stupa against his better judgement.

Meanwhile the arrogant and foolhardy Narathihapati had begun to fall foul of the Mongols. Master of an empire stretching from the Yellow Sea to the Carpathians, Kublai Khan had already annexed Yunnan and Nanchao. He then sent word through his governor in Yunnan, and when this was ignored, despatched an Imperial delegation to the court of Pagan demanding 'golden ricepots, vessels, basins and ladles of silver and gold' and, according to some chronicles, even a white elephant – in other words, Burma's submission as a tributary state. In presenting their demands, the ambassadors neglected to conform to Burmese royal protocol, further infuriating Narathahapati, who ordered that they be put to death. His ministers cautioned: 'Although the ambassadors have behaved ill in their ignorance of royal ceremony . . . speak conciliatory words . . . The kings of old were never wont to kill ambassadors. Be advised, therefore, and endure.' Narathihapati was, however, adamant, and the ambassadors were executed. Then, to add insult to injury, he attacked his two northern neighbours, who had submitted to the Mongols.

Marco Polo gives an account of the conflict in which Narathihapati is routed and put to flight despite the vast superiority in numbers of the Burmese and their army of elephants (63).

The defeated Burmese forces fell back towards Pagan and began to prepare for a siege. In its early days Pagan had been a walled town, and a small portion of the old wall, together with the Sarabha Gateway survives to this day. But during the subsequent period of political stability, fortifications had seemed unnecessary for a capital glorying in the title of Arimaddanapura (The City that Tramples its Enemies Underfoot). Now, in the frantic rush to erect a barrier in the face of the advancing Mongols, some ten thousand temples and stupas were demolished for their materials. In the foundation of one of the desecrated holy places, relates The Glass Palace Chronicle, a copper plate was found, inscribed with the prophecy: 'In the reign of a king who is father of twins, the Kingdom of Pagan will utterly perish at the hands of the Tarops (Chinese). When the superstitious Narathihapati found to his consternation that one of his young concubines had, indeed, recently given birth to twins, he lost heart and lamented: 'Albeit I build a town in my defence, I cannot defend it.' And Narathihapati abandoned his great capital without a struggle and fled south to Bassein, earning for himself the contemptuous

74 Bas-relief on a pavilion of the Baphuon, Angkor, Cambodia

epithet of 'The king who fled from the Chinese'.

On this ignominious note the most glorious chapter in the history of Burma ended, with Pagan added to the long list of kingdoms destroyed by the Mongols (64). Although Burma was spared the pyramids of skulls and smoking ruins that marked the progress of the Mongols elsewhere, and although the occupation lasted a relatively brief fifteen years, the dissolution of the Pagan dynasty in 1287 dealt a blow from which the country never fully recovered. Political unity was not achieved again for centuries, and Burmese culture never again reached the heights it had attained during the Pagan Period.

The great city, considered ill-omened, was abandoned and the secular buildings of light construction decayed, leaving only the religious edifices. Still today, the spires of no less than five thousand pagodas, scattered over an area of sixteen square miles, rise from the sun-scorched plain where peasants herd their cattle among the scrubby cactus and euphorbia.

Almost the sole relic of the Mongol occupation of Pagan is the series of frescoes in the Kyanzittha Monastery. These include a representation of a Mongolian officer with typical Tartar features: almond eyes, high cheekbones, wispy moustache and sparse beard, holding a falcon – a method of hunting never practised in Burma as far as is known. The most evocative painting and the most interesting aesthetically, is that of a monk of Central-Asian type telling his prayer beads (Plate 51), one member at least of his race to succumb to the gentle creed of the Buddha.

A fitting epilogue is provided by the decorations dating from the Ava Dynasty (17th and 18th centuries) in a few structures still occupied by monks at this late period (Plates 57 and 58). Utterly charming in their colourful, folk-art tradition, they also serve as a poignant reminder of the lost grandeur of the earlier epoch.

75 Vertiginous stairway and angle tower of the central shrine, Angkor Wat, Cambodia

76 The Naga King protects the Devaraja in the guise of the meditating Buddha from the 'Cosmic Storm'; statue in the style of Angkor Wat. *Musée Guimet, Paris*

3 Angkor *The Abode of the God-King*

The flight to Angkor from Phnom Penh sets the key-note for the saga of the Khmers of Cambodia. Great rivers meander seemingly aimlessly over the flat land, connected by a continuous, silver filigree of interlacing canals, broadening into ponds and lakes and culminating in the vast expanse of the Great Lake of the Tonle Sap, stretching to the very horizon – a land almost submerged; apt setting for a culture dominated and obsessed by water.

A Chinese emissary in the middle of the third century A.D. provides the first account of the legend of the foundation of the early kingdom of Funan. Kaundinya, a Brahmin of noble birth, landed from a merchant ship, married the daughter of the native ruler, a *naga* king, and became master of the land. To provide a fitting dowry for his daughter, the serpent-king drank the water inundating the land so that his progeny might cultivate the soil.

We have here a particularly succinct allegory of the process of Hinduization of 'Greater India': trader-missionaries in the outposts of the Indian mercantile empire consolidated their power through local alliances and introduced the fruits of Indian culture, including superior irrigation techniques by means of which uninhabitable mangrove swamps were drained and new land made available for cultivation.

Scholars are inclined to place the arrival of Kaundinya – or the rise of the first 'Hinduized' state in Indo-China – not later than the first century A.D. (65). At this period the settlements along the banks of the lower Mekong River and its tributaries, the home of man since Neolithic times, formed part of the Austro-Asiatic (or Malayo-Polynesian) civilization, centred in the region of the South-China Sea, and extending to the far islands of the archipelago. Despite the immense distances involved, this culture was remarkably homogenous, manifesting basically the same characteristics everywhere. Its achievements included a knowledge of rice-cultivation in paddy-fields, and the strong social organization necessary to undertake irrigation projects entailing mass labour; the domestication of the ox and buffalo; a rudimentary knowledge of metals – though the fine stone tools also continued in use – and great skill in navigation. Beliefs were a compound of ancestor-worship, animism and chthonic cults, manifested in a mythology which stressed the cosmological dualism of Earth versus Water, Mountain versus Sea and Winged Beings versus Water Beings, the latter expressed in the antagonism between the Solar Bird and the *Naga* Serpent (66). To prove of singular significance was the practice of locating shrines on high places. South-East Asia thus already possessed a civilization of its own when the first waves of Indian influence were felt. Modern scholars are attributing ever greater importance to this fact in explaining the marked divergence between the cultures developed in South-East Asia under Indian tutelage and the parent culture. Certain mores, firmly established at this date, even though apparently suppressed, continued to lie dormant beneath the mantle of Indian culture and reasserted themselves at an opportune time; others limited the aspects of Indian culture which were acceptable. A striking instance is afforded by the elevated status of women in Austro-Asiatic society where both descent and inheritance were in the female line. This was so deeply ingrained that the subjugation of women prescribed by Hindu custom was flatly rejected – despite the prestige attaching to all things Indian – and women continued to play a prominent role in public life, even occupying such positions as professor and judge during the great days of Angkor, as we shall see.

To these shores and this Austro-Asiatic culture came the first major wave of Indian influence at the turn of our era. This was the beginning of the golden age of maritime contacts in the region, with Indian merchants plying their trade in the spices and other precious products of the East, so in demand at the luxurious courts of the Roman Empire, as far as the ports of South China. The area of the lower Mekong River was most conveniently located in relation to this trade, particularly when the dangers of the narrow Malacca and Sunda Straits, infested with pirates, led to the widespread use of land portage across the narrow Isthmus of Kra of the Malay Peninsula. The area was also the converging point of several important land trade routes from the north and west.

The first centuries A.D. saw the rise of the first great state of Indo-China, the Kingdom of Funan, with its capital of Vyadhapura, or 'The City of Hunters', situated on a bank of the Mekong some hundred and twenty miles from the sea, and its chief port of Oc Eo at the river-mouth, on the Gulf of Siam. The ruins of Oc Eo have been excavated, revealing a vast urban agglomeration of pile-dwellings. A highly complex network of canals and sewers, extending for over twenty miles, drained the stagnant swamp waters into the sea and reclaimed the land for agriculture.

Funan prospered greatly. By the middle of the third century its ruler was sending embassies to India and China, the latter with a gift of musicians and native products. A few years later China sent a return mission including K'ang T'ai who recorded the earliest extant account of the country, and narrated the legend of Kaundinya. He observed that the capital was walled and its chief buildings of brick covered with stucco, while the common people lived in simple dwellings of bamboo raised on piles in settlements often protected only by wooden palisades. The people, he noted, were 'ugly, black and frizzy-haired', probably indicative of a strong Negrito or Melanesoid strain, and were naked above the waist. K'ang T'ai claimed that previously the men had gone completely naked and that he, personally, had influenced the ruler of Funan to issue a decree ordering them to wear a loin-cloth, the origin of the Cambodian *sampot*. The same had earlier been done for women by Kaundinya, who seems to have been something of a prude. He not only made his *nagini* bride wear clothing, but also made her do her hair in a top-knot.

Cotton and sugar-cane were grown in addition to rice. Taxes were paid in precious metals, pearls or aromatic woods, and records were written in an Indian script and kept in archives. Justice was primitive: trial by ordeal often being resorted to. Artisans worked not only in stone but also in silver and gold and were particularly skilled in chasing and engraving techniques. Traffic was by boat, utilizing a system of canals so extensive that the Chinese could talk of 'sailing *across* Funan'. Cock- and pig-fights were popular amusements. The name 'Funan' was given to the country by the Chinese. It was derived from the title of the ruler *kurung bnam* or 'King of the Mountain'. What the real name was, we shall probably never know.

Funan developed imperial dimensions – and pretensions – by the third century and reached its peak at the beginning of the fifth century when traffic through the Straits had dwindled to a mere trickle and the portage-traffic across the Malay Peninsula enjoyed a virtual monopoly. At this stage the empire of Funan extended over most of present-day Cambodia, Cochin-China and portions of the Malay Peninsula, and exerted a measure of sovereignty over a host of vassal states, among them the Mon Kingdom of Thaton.

It was peopled chiefly by the Mon-Khmer tribes of South Chinese origin, to which had been added foreign strains, mainly Indian. These more sophisticated elements were superimposed on a substream of primitive aborigines – the 'fuzzy-haired' people mentioned by the Chinese chroniclers – who were destined to be enslaved or take refuge ever further in the mountains and forests.

'ig. 12 Stone colossus in the jungle, Cambodia; engraving from *Voyage 'exploration en Indo-chine*, by Francis Garnier, 1873

Among the kingdoms tributary to Funan was the Khmer state of Chenla, centred around Bassac in present-day, Southern Laos. Although racially closely akin to the Funanese, the Mon-Khmers of Chenla traced their ancestry to an independent source: the union of a mythical ascetic, Kambu, and an *apsaras*, or celestial nymph, named Mera, who were considered to have founded a 'Solar Dynasty' – in contradistinction to the 'Lunar Dynasty' of Funan. They called themselves 'Sons of Kambu' or *Kambuja*, hence the name Cambodia.

Chenla started its rise to prominence during the fifth century, and by the beginning of the sixth had become virtually independent. As the century progressed there was general unrest in Funan following disastrous floods which forced the abandonment of much of the reclaimed area of Cochin-China; and bitter dynastic disputes culminating in the reign of a usurper. In the year 540, a Funanese prince married to a princess of Chenla – and hence uniting both Solar and Lunar Dynasties – took advantage of the confusion, swept down on the old capital and seized power for Chenla.

The new rulers continued along the lines of cultural development set by Funan, adopting the customary Funanese honorific, Indian suffix: *varman*, meaning protégé. Thus, Indravarman, for example, signifies 'He who is under the protection of the God Indra'.

The new rulers were initially unable to exercise control over the whole of their vast inheritance and many of the more distant tributary states assumed independence. The seventh century, though turbulent, saw the gradual consolidation of Chenla's power, but in the early years of the eighth century she in turn fell prey to disruptive forces from within which split the country into two kingdoms: 'Chenla of the Land' in the north, centred around the former Khmer state, and 'Chenla of the Sea', occupying the nucleus of Funan proper.

Meanwhile there had been a general shift of power in South-East Asia to the South, with the rise of the splendid 'Island Empires' of Sumatra and Java. Their origin is shrouded in mystery and has been the subject of much speculation. One of the most intriguing hypotheses connects the great Sailendra Dynasty of Java with the royal house of Funan, members of which may have fled to Java after the conquest of their empire by Chenla.

The eighth century is, perhaps, the most obscure in the history of Cambodia. Little is known for certain, particularly of 'Chenla of the Land'. 'Chenla of the Water' split into several small kingdoms owing only nominal allegiance to their most powerful member, and towards the end of the century became a vassal of the Sailendra Dynasty of Java.

Sulayman, a ninth century Arab voyager to these shores, related an interesting tale pertaining to the fall of Chenla (67). The youthful Khmer ruler, envious of his great neighbour, the Maharaja of Zabag (Java), expressed the wish to see his rival's head on a platter. His chief minister was horrified and warned him to keep his desire secret. The king retorted by proclaiming it publicly. When word reached the Javanese ruler, he, though loath to take any action, realized that the insult would have to be punished. On the pretext of undertaking a tour of his island domains, he equipped a large naval force and landed secretly on the coast of Chenla. He took the Khmers by surprise and captured their capital and monarch. Before the assembled notables of Chenla the victor pronounced judgement on the young king: 'Should you have wished to seize my empire or reduce it to ruins, I would have done the same to your country. However, since you merely wished to see my head on a platter, I shall do to you what you intended for me; and then return to my country without taking anything belonging to the land of Khmer.' He was as good as his word. Except for the foolish young man's head – which he subsequently had embalmed and returned in an urn as a warning to his successor – he took no booty. He even rewarded the old counsellor for attempting to dissuade the young king from his folly, and instructed the ministers to choose a new king. 'This,' concluded the Arab chronicler, 'is the reason why the kings of the Khmers, on rising, prostrate themselves in the direction of Java and do homage to its great ruler.'

We have here, obviously a Javanese version of events and, as in the case of Anawrahta's expedition against Thaton, we cannot but be suspicious of an alleged provocation which induced a power in the ascendant to exert its authority over a weaker neighbour. The main events are, however, corroborated by external evidence. We know that the Sailendras of Java undertook a successful expedition against Chenla to avenge an insult, executed the king and installed on the throne a Khmer prince, approved by the Maharaja and dependent on Java.

The young prince chosen was Jayavarman II. He was not in the main line of succession, and had evidently spent his youth at the Sailendra court – whether as guest, exile or hostage is not clear. After his coronation, Jayavarman II systematically consolidated his hold over Lower Chenla in a series of military expeditions, operating from a new frontier-capital as base each time. When he had established a firm footing in the readily-defensible area of Angkor at the head of the Great Lake of the Tonle Sap in the middle Mekong region, he proclaimed his independence of Java with a bold and dramatic gesture that ushered in a new era in the history of Cambodia. He adopted the supreme title of 'King of the Mountain' and solemnized the act with a religious ceremony. A great stone lingam, symbol of the creative energy of the god, Siva, was erected on the summit of Phnom Kulen, a hill near Angkor, and by means of an esoteric ritual conducted by a Brahmin 'skilled in magic science', the king was transformed into an incarnation of the god, manifest in the form of the *Devaraja* or 'God-King'. The 'Divine Essence of Kingship' or sacral personality of the king would henceforth reside in the royal lingam. The whole ceremony, we learn from an inscription, was conducted 'to the express purpose that the land of Kambuja should be freed from dependence on Java and be ruled by a sole sovereign who should be a *Cakravartin* or "World Ruler".'

In order to understand the significance of this ceremony and its efficacy as an instrument of royal power, a broad picture of the religious scene in Cambodia is necessary. K'ang T'ai, in his description of third century Funan, reported that the ruler 'honoured the Buddha'. A couple of centuries later found Buddhism and the Hindu cults of Siva and Vishnu coexisting in tolerant amity. The Chinese tribute

77 Apsaras, Angkor Wat, Cambodia

7

7

mission of Jayavarman I of Funan (478-514) 'praised in successive breaths the advantages of the Saivite cult in reducing the population to submission and the Buddhist propagation of mercy and compassion to all', (68), while his queen was the author of a famed invocation to Vishnu, couched in perfect Sanskrit.

Siva was from this period on generally the patron deity of the realm. God of both Creation and Destruction, it was his beneficent aspect which was stressed in south-East Asia, in the phallic cult of *Sivalinga*. This, too, was the form dominant in Java where the lingam became the symbol of royal power – hence the pertinence of Jayavarman II's gesture of defiance.

We have seen that the early Austro-Asiatic culture attached great significance to placing shrines on high, and this belief was reinforced by the Hindu cosmological myth which located the abode of the gods on the summit of Mount Meru, at the epicentre of the universe. This was to have as consequence the conviction that stable government demanded the elevation of the state *lingam* of the *Devaraja* on a mountain – natural or artificial – situated at the exact centre of the universe as determined by the Brahmin astrologers.

The cult of the *Devaraja* initiated by Jayavarman II, together with its associated deification of the royal ancestors, was to assume paramount importance in the culture of Angkor. It provided the mystical basis for the absolute power of the Khmer ruler, worshipped as both king and god, and supplied the motivation to erect structures unsurpassed in grandeur and scale even by the pharaohs. What is more, the temple-mountain of each king became his mausoleum at his death and could not be used by his successor to perform the rites necessary to enlist the co-operation of the chthonic deities on whose benevolence the rice-crop, and hence the very existence of the nation, depended. Hence each sovereign had to erect a new 'god-mountain'. Culturally, this ensured a continuity of architectural and decorative traditions and left one of the richest artistic legacies of mankind. Economically, the growing profusion of temples involving an enormous expenditure on both construction and maintenance, imposed a crushing burden which was eventually to prove disastrous.

The move to the Angkor region was to prove momentous. Situated at the furthest navigable point from the sea, it was at the same time conveniently accessible and seemed free from the danger of surprise attack. Natural resources were plentiful: timber and game – especially that *sine qua non*, the elephant – from the forests; sandstone eminently suitable for construction from the quarries of Phnom Kulen and the Dangrek Mountains to the north, and iron in sufficient quantities for a non-industrial society. An abundant water supply and the extremely fertile soil of the alluvial plain ensured ideal conditions for cultivation, but this combination also obtained elsewhere.

What made the choice of the Angkor region so felicitous was that it enabled the Khmers to take full advantage of a natural phenomenon. The great lake is connected by means of the Tonle Sap River with the Mekong which, at the site of the present capital of Phnom Penh further downstream, splits its two branches. When the snows of the Himalayas melt and heavy rains upstream send the Mekong down in flood, these two branches are unable to receive the swirling mass of water. The water then backs up the Tonle Sap, causing its flow to be reversed and the Great Lake becomes a vast reservoir, expanding to three times its normal size and flooding large areas. When, some months later, the floodwaters of the Mekong subside, the Tonle Sap once again resumes its normal flow, draining the overflow of the Great Lake. Millions of fish, fattened on the rich vegetation of the submerged

78 The colonnaded gallery of Angkor Wat, Cambodia

79 Life-size bas-relief from the 'Elephant Terrace', Angkor Thom, Cambodia

forest – making the Lake the world's richest natural fish preserve – are trapped in the muddy shallows and can easily be caught. Salted and preserved, fish constitutes the chief addition to the Cambodian staple diet of rice.

Jayavarman II laid the practical foundation for the prosperity of Angkor by initiating the elaborate irrigation system. With the transfer to the region of the Great Lake, a new approach to irrigation had become necessary. In the low-lying delta areas the chief problem had been the drainage of swampy ground; now it was to conserve water during the torrential monsoon rains for distribution during the dry months. Unlike the setting for the great classical civilization of Ceylon, there was no actual shortage of water, hence the problem was, in essence, simpler. The solution was to create great catchment basins known as *barays* formed by building embankments or dykes rather than excavating the ground. A triple system of dykes around not merely the city, but the entire district, guarded against inundation during the annual flooding of the Tonle Sap. At such times Angkor must have seemed an island marooned among the waters. The appearance of isolation would, however, be illusory, for water transportation probably always remained the chief form of communication. To this end, reservoirs and canals were interconnected to form a vast and co-ordinated system of waterworks (69), of which even the monumental moats which surrounded the great temples formed an integral part. This final stage of perfection was only reached several centuries after the time of Jayavarman II, coinciding with the Golden Age of Angkor. It has been mentioned here so that the twin bases on which the culture of Angkor was built: the mystical cult of the *Devaraja* and an ingenious and eminently practical irrigation system, can be considered in conjunction. The divine ruler commands the implicit obedience of the masses necessary to undertake the enormous irrigation works. These, in turn, make possible the harvesting of three or even four annual crops, the basis for the astounding agricultural wealth of Angkor and the support of the vast population required to wage aggressive wars of expansion and Empire, and to construct the incomparable monuments of Angkor which in their turn reflect the glory of the *Devaraja*, increasing yet further his prestige, bolstering his power and bringing the chain full-cycle.

Recent research would seem to indicate a far closer connection between religious and secular structures than was first thought. It appears that each ruler was expected to undertake works for the common weal before commencing the temple-mountain to house his sacred lingam. Inscriptions speak of 'a holy barrage causing the water to flow where previously there was none' . . . and of a reservoir 'beautiful as the moon, built to refresh mankind and to drown the insolence of other kings'. The use of the epithet 'holy' is significant. It appears that no temple was built without its great ponds which must have been both practical and beautiful. Thus, as in Ancient Egypt, the divine and mundane were inextricably connected. In both cases the seemingly boundless energy of a great people would be channelled into the creation of works of cyclopean magnitude.

A comparison between the 'tanks' of Ceylon and the *barays* of Angkor is revealing. The 'tanks', which could hardly be called by a name less indicative of their character, are in reality lakes of irregular outline, reflecting the natural contours in an organic way. With their tree-covered bunds they might almost be works of nature. They provide an informal and romantic setting for the great stupas reminiscent almost of the landscaped backdrop for the English country house devised by Capability Brown and his school. The *barays* of Angkor on the contrary are pristinely geometric and architectonic, and of a formal splendour which would not have put Le Notre to shame. At Angkor, as at Versailles, we have a landscape imposed upon nature by man. The fact that temple-mountains and the system of waterworks – *barays*, canals and moats – are identical in character, together forming an integral and indissoluble whole, provides the key to an understanding of their full significance. The waterworks of Angkor were not decorative or even merely 'practical' – in the narrow sense of the word. They were 'practical' also in the sense that they were essential to the efficient functioning of a cosmological scheme of magic calculated to ensure the prosperity of the realm.

As in Ceylon, the precision displayed in the lay-out of irrigation works is astounding. A moat more than two miles in length showed a maximum error of half an inch, for example, while a canal was found to run perfectly for thirty miles – measured by the most accurate modern instruments.

The jungle-covered remains of the temples built by Jayavarman II on the summit of Mount Kulen are transitional in style. Not surprisingly, they reveal strong Javanese influences, superimposed upon the Indianized style of the pre-Angkorean Khmer monuments.

It was left to Jayavarman's successors to impose political unity on the entire country and develop the 'Style of Angkor'. During his long reign Jayavarman II moved the capital successively to several different sites. His capital of Hariharalaya (70) was near the present village of Roluos some fourteen miles south-east of Angkor, and served as the royal seat under several of his successors. It is the monuments dating from this period, constituting the so-called 'Roluos Group', that herald a new style of architecture and decoration, very different from what had gone before and serving as the point of departure for subsequent developments.

Indravarman I (877-889) built the Bakong, the first of the artificial 'god-mountains' of Angkor, as the main temple of the capital. Situated on flat ground, the 'mountain' rises in the form of a stepped-pyramid of five tiers crowned by a central sanctuary. Around the base of the pyramid are grouped isolated brick tower-shrines, and disposed on either side of the main approach from the east are two small pavilions of stone, of a type that was to become a familiar feature of the great temples. They are called 'libraries' for convenience. Their actual use is unknown, but they may well have been used to store ritual accessories, sacred books or the temple archives. The complex is enclosed by a girdle wall pierced by four entrances, each of which is defined by pavilions, and a wide moat surrounds the entire temple area. At the Bakong for the first time, the major part of the structure – the pyramidal mass – was built of stone. The present central tower appears to be a late twelfth-century restoration. Among the most attractive features of the Bakong today are the elegant brick towers of unassuming scale and conventional brick construction (Plate 60). The door lintels and the three 'false doors' carved in stone, simulating the single door of wood and metal, which originally gave access to the interior from the east, are outstanding for the quality of their decoration – of an almost Churrigeresque exuberance (Plate 87).

The neighbouring temple of Preah Ko also dates from the same reign. The stucco relief illustrated (Plate 66), clearly inspired by a wood-carving tradition, is typical of the decoration of this small but exquisite temple. The 'glory-head' or ogre disgorging foliate motifs may with profit be compared with a similar motif from Pagan (Plate 42) The supreme dexterity and dynamism of the Angkor example will immediately be apparent.

Indravarman's son and successor, Yasovarman I (889-900), built the first city at Angkor proper, which he named Yasodharapura in his own honour. Henceforth the capital – for 'Angkor' is a corrupted form of the Sanskrit *nagara*, or 'capital city' – would be increasingly identified with the Empire of the Khmers. In this respect the use of 'Angkor' might well be compared with the Roman use of *Urbs* as referring to the Eternal City (71).

The pre-eminence of Angkor must not blind us to the fact that splendid cities and monuments also arose elsewhere. Among these was the great temple of Preah Vihear, high in the Dangrek Mountains on the present border with Thailand. Probably built by Yasovarman I, it exhibits a profound sensitivity in exploiting the potential drama of one of the most spectacular sites in the world. A highly complex combination of pools, causeway and seemingly endless stairs climbs a gentle incline – the outlook all the while deliberately constricted – and terminates at the temple proper, perched on the very edge of a sheer precipice 2300 ft. high.

A similar recognition of the possibilities offered by a natural feature seems to have precipitated the momentous move from nearby Roluos to the present site of Angkor. In this case the inducement was a hill some two-hundred feet high whose inclination made it ideally suited to conversion into a temple-mountain with a minimum of labour. The result was the temple of Phnom Bakheng, a milestone in the evolution of Khmer architecture.

Here, for the first time, the topmost level of the temple-mountain was crowned by not one but five towers, the highest in the middle and lower ones at each of the four corners, symbolizing the five peaks of sacred Mount Meru. This quincuncial arrangement would become a characteristic feature, and one to which classical Khmer architecture would owe much of its liveliness of silhouette. Unfortunately at Phnom Bakheng only the central tower remains; those defining the corners being reduced to ruin, so that the original effect cannot be properly comprehended. From the summit there is a magnificent view of the jungle and the towers of Angkor Wat.

Yasovarman I ruled over a large empire. Precisely how large, and what proportion was inherited and what due to Yasovarman's much-vaunted skill as a warrior and conqueror, has been a subject of much speculation and controversy. According to inscriptions, his empire was as extensive as that of Funan at her zenith: stretching from the border of China on the north, Champa (in present-day South Vietnam) on the east, the Indian Ocean on the west, and including the northern portion of the Malay Peninsula. Some modern scholars concur with this; others would exclude domination of the Mon Kingdom of Thaton and the upper Malay Peninsula. Even so it was an Empire not unworthy of the pretensions of the *Cakravartin* title.

The greatest achievement of Yasovarman I was, however, in the field of irrigation. He endowed his new capital with a vast network of reservoirs, pools and moats, including the immense East Baray with a capacity of over a thousand million gallons.

Two important monuments dating from the middle years of the tenth century serve as exemplars of the main lines of development of Khmer religious architecture at the time. In the temple of Baksei Chamrong, of modest scale but superb proportions and elegance, we have the classic expression of the temple-mountain reduced to absolute essentials: a steep four-tiered pyramid of laterite surmounted by a single brick shrine (Plate 63). The apparent simplicity is, however, deceptive, concealing a number of highly sophisticated refinements. The precipitous stairs climbing the centre of each face of the pyramid, for example, diminish in width as

80 Cavalry officers; detail of the great gallery bas-relief, Angkor Wat, Cambodia

81 Portion of the team of gods holding the sacred serpent; detail of the 'Churning of the Sea of Milk', Angkor Wat, Cambodia

they ascend, a deliberate falsification of perspective which here, as in Bernini's *Scala Regia* of the Vatican, gives an effect of added depth in space and a heightened sense of monumentality. The almost cubist purity of the volumes has been enhanced by the destruction of the original elaborate plaster decoration. An inscription on the piers of the brick sanctuary bears a date corresponding to 947, during the reign of Rajendravarman II and mentions the erection of a cult image of Siva in pure gold.

The Temple of Pre Rup is far larger and more complex in layout. The top terrace of the pyramidal mass has the characteristic quincuncial arrangement of five towers. Here for the last time in a large temple, the shrines were built of brick. Henceforth they, too, would be constructed of stone. The stairways ascending the pyramid of Pre Rup are remarkable for their particularly fine guardian lions (Plate 55).

The tenth century saw a consolidation of Khmer power and a growing cultural maturity. The chief political event was a usurpation of power marked by a temporary removal of the capital to Koh Ker some hundred miles to the north-east. The subsequent return was final. Angkor remained the capital as long as the empire of the Khmers endured.

From the reign of Jayavarman V (968-1001) dates the temple of Banteay Srei, or 'The Citadel of the Women'. Small but gem-like, it would be the obvious choice if one were asked to name the most endearing monument of all Angkor.

Banteay Srei stands alone, some thirteen miles to the north of Angkor. The sandy country road – quite impassable in the rainy season – passes through a typical Cambodian landscape, forest and brush alternating with rice fields, always presided over by at least one group of tall palms which sway and rustle in the slightest breeze.

The temple of Banteay Srei rises from a low platform, the felicitous and unique warm-pink hue of the sandstone singularly effective against the background of great trees. Although the total complex covers a considerable area, the individual structures – gateway pavilions, shrines and 'libraries' – are of almost diminutive scale. The shrine doorways, for example, are no more than five feet high. But as if to compensate for this reduced compass, the decoration is of the utmost lavishness. The earliest religious architecture of Cambodia, and secular buildings throughout the Angkor period, were of wood. This influence is particularly evident at Banteay Srei, where the minute decoration covering every square inch harks back to a wood-carving tradition. The quality throughout is superlative – a spiral ornament terminating the angle of a gable being executed with the care one would normally associate with figure-sculpture (Plate 69). Guarding the entrances to the shrines are unique lion-, ape- and bird-headed figures, crouching on one knee. They are placed so as to accent and animate most successfully the small courts created by the placing of the five main buildings (Plate 59). Some of the *dvarapalas* are heavily encrusted with lichen, increasing yet further their bizarre appearance (Plate 67). In striking contrast are the benign deities, male and female, enshrined in niches in the shrine walls (Plates 61 and 62). In these figures can be seen a peculiarity of figure sculpture throughout the Angkor period: that, whereas the greatest skill and sensitivity is evident in the treatment of the head, arms and torso, there is a marked falling-off in quality below the waist, almost as if this work had been relegated to an inferior hand (72). Curiously enough, the least attractive feature of the modern Cambodian is his short legs and thick-set ankle joints. The sculptors of Banteay Srei reserved their greatest triumphs for the elaborate tympana or gable pediments. Here for the first time, we find themes from Hindu mythology rendered in narrative

82 Apsaras, Angkor Wat, Cambodia

83 A chorus of Apsarases, Angkor Wat, Cambodia

Fig. 13 Principal façade of Angkor Wat; engraving from *Voyage d'exploration en Indo-chine*, by Francis Garnier, 1873

fashion – an art form in which the Khmers were to achieve incomparable heights.

Exceptional both for its beauty and perfect state of preservation is the tympanum in the Museé Guimet depicting the demons Sounda and Aupasounda disputing possession of the *Apsaras*, Tilottama (Plate 65).

The demons were causing great havoc – completely disrupting the order of the Universe – so the gods sent this celestial damsel to entice them both and incite them to jealousy. On the pediment the *apsaras* stands calmly between the two club-brandishing rivals – presumably assured of divine protection – while the prayers of prospective victims and two heavenly beings hovering overhead encourage the 'beneficent' conflict which ended in the mutual destruction of the demons. Not the least attractive feature of this masterpiece of decorative sculpture is the band of delicately carved ornament whose rhythmic convolutions enclose the characteristic trilobate gable form. It terminates at the two ends in *makara* heads disgorging rampant *nagas*. Above, foliate motifs terminate in flamboyant cresting reminiscent of Pagan. Another magnificent tympanum, still *in situ*, is that on the east face of the north 'library', depicting Indra, the Thunder God, on his tricephalous elephant, sending down beneficent rains on a rejoicing animal and plant kingdom (Plate 68). Monkeys disport amid the superbly decorative stone foliage of the forest trees, and above rises a flock of birds, eager to enjoy the refreshing rain. This is represented by a multitude of straight lines on which is superimposed a king *naga*, presiding by right over his element: water.

The beginning of the eleventh century saw the accession of one of the greatest kings of Angkor: Suryavarman I. He was the son of the king of Tambralinga, a small state on the Malay Peninsula which had only recently declared its independence of Srivijayan Sumatra. Taking advantage of the disputed succession following the death of Jayavarman V, the warlike young prince claimed the throne for himself, through his mother, a Khmer princess. Only after a bloody struggle

Fig. 14 Lower cloistered gallery, Angkor Wat; engraving from *Voyage d'exploration en Indo-chine*, by Francis Garnier, 1873

lasting all but a decade, was he finally successful in 'breaking the circle of his enemies'. As Suryavarman I (1002-1050) he reigned for almost half a century. He was a ruler of exceptional ability. 'In his skill as a warrior, organizer and ruler, his fine spirit of toleration, his habit of surrounding himself with scholarly and high-minded advisers, his patronage of art and architecture and his promotion of public improvements, he rates high among the kings of Ancient Cambodia – perhaps the highest' (73). Although personally a Mahayana Buddhist, he no doubt felt that a change of the state religion might undermine its stability and strengthened yet further the *Devaraja* cult, emphasizing its political aspects. At the same time he assured freedom of worship for both Hinayana and Mahayana Buddhists. An inscription surviving from his reign records the oath of allegiance sworn by the chief dignitaries of the realm, some four thousand in number: 'Our lives are dedicated to His Majesty up to the day of our death . . . We shall not honour any other king, ever be the accomplices of any enemy, or seek to injure His Majesty in any way . . . If there is war, we pledge ourselves to fight faithfully in his cause without valuing our lives . . . If His Majesty orders us to go abroad to ascertain any matter, we shall seek to learn everything about it . . . If all of us who are here present do not uphold this oath of allegiance to His Majesty, may he yet reign long and inflict all measure of punishment upon us. If we hide ourselves to avoid carrying out the oath, may we be reborn in the thirty-two Hells as long as the sun and the moon abide . . . But if we loyally keep our promise, may His Majesty give orders for the upkeep of the pious foundations of our country and for the maintenance of our families . . . And may we obtain the reward due to faithful servants in this world and the next.' Interestingly enough, the oath of allegiance sworn at the coronation of the modern kings of Cambodia is almost identical, a most striking example of historical continuity, especially considering that the very existence of Angkor had been all but forgotten a century ago.

With the help of his father, still reigning in Tambralinga, Suryavarman I conquered the eastern Mon kingdoms of the Menam Valley and Korat Plateau, thus adding to the Khmer Empire a large part of present-day Thailand. This disruption of the Mon Confederacy coincided with the rise of the Burmese Kingdom of Pagan and no doubt greatly facilitated Anawrahta's conquest of the Mon Kingdom of Thaton shortly afterwards.

A vast extension to the irrigation system is credited to Suryavarman's reign and constitutes one of his greatest claims to fame. In the field of architecture he limited himself to the completion and decoration of structures commenced by his immediate predecessors. Chief among these was the temple of Takeo, a gigantic 'god-mountain' culminating in the customary quincunx, the central tower being no less than two hundred feet high. It incorporated stone galleries along its terraces, an innovation whose great significance in the development of Khmer architecture we shall consider later.

The second major monument was the Phimeanakas which formed the focal point of the vast palace complex. This very unusual stone pyramid with extremely steep sides and vertiginous access stairs had a stone gallery running around the perimeter of the topmost terrace and a single tower. This was the reputed scene of one of the strangest of all Khmer rituals. In this 'tower of gold' – a reference, no doubt, to the practice of gilding towers introduced by Suryavarman I under western influence – dwelt a nine-headed serpent, daughter of the King of the Nagas. Each night on the arrival of the Khmer ruler, the serpent took the form of a beautiful damsel. Only after the sovereign had consorted with her, was he free to leave and sleep with his wives and concubines. The people believed that if the king failed to consort with the naga-princess, a great misfortune would befall the kingdom. If on the other hand, the naga-princess failed to appear, this heralded the imminent death of the sovereign.

The ceremony perpetuates the legend of the founding-father of the Empire of Funan, Kaundinya, and his naga-princess, Soma, and symbolizes the union of the God-King and the guardian of the beneficent waters so essential to the prosperity of the land.

The most important monument of the second half of the eleventh century was the gigantic Baphuon, located just outside the high wall which surrounded the entire palace complex. With its five terraces and three concentric, stone-vaulted galleries, the pavilions accenting the corners of the terraces and its magnificent entrance gateways, it anticipated many of the features of Angkor Wat. Unfortunately, subsidence of the foundation has caused the collapse of large portions of the structure.

Perhaps the most delightful feature of the Baphuon is its superb decorative sculpture (Plates 72 and 74). This includes not only the usual elaborate floriate motifs, executed with consummate skill, but also a large number of narrative scenes. These are no longer confined to focal points as at Banteay Srei, but spread over large wall surfaces. It is precisely in some of the more obscure nooks and angles where, like the mediaeval sculptor, the Khmer artist felt he could safely indulge his fancy, that we find some of the most enchanting vignettes, notably of animals.

The reign of Suryavarman II (1113-1150) ushered in the Golden Age of the Khmer Empire, both politically and culturally. A most able ruler and statesman, he was also a renowned warrior and expanded the boundaries of the Empire further than ever before. For a brief period the ruler of Angkor, with the sole exception of

84 Detail of a door lintel at Preah Ko. The fabulous animal is a Makara, here portrayed without the usual dolphin tail; 'Roluos Group', Angkor, Cambodia

85 Village scene from a bas-relief at the Bayon, Angkor Thom, Cambodia

86 A giant silk-cotton tree sprouts from the roof of a shrine at the Temple of Ta Prohm, its blanched roots holding the stone in a living vice; Angkor, Cambodia

87 'False Door' in stone of a tower-shrine at the Bakong. The elaborate sandstone lintel is typical of the period; 'Roluos Group', Angkor, Cambodia

90

91

the Emperor of China, was the greatest potentate in Asia. The patron deity of Suryavarman II was Vishnu and it is ironical that 'The Preserver', nearly always subordinate to Siva 'The Creator and Destroyer' during the long history of the Khmers, should have had the greatest monument of Angkor – and, indeed, in all Asia – dedicated in his honour: the Temple of Angkor Wat. This was not only the royal sanctuary of the king as *Devaraja* – in this case, strictly-speaking, *Vishnuraja*, the cult-image being not a lingam but a gold statue of the god Vishnu astride his winged mount, Garuda. It also served as Suryavarman's mausoleum.

Though many Khmer temples seem to have fulfilled both these functions, at Angkor Wat alone were the death-centred attributes triumphant and paramount. Thus, it alone is oriented not towards the source of light and life, the east; but towards the west, the direction associated with the setting sun, darkness and death. Its location, too, was unusual; not the centre of the capital but placed somewhat apart, as if in deference to the Hindu precept that the dead should not dwell with the living. To these unusual characteristics must also be added the inimitable nature of a supreme masterpiece. At Angkor Wat, as at the Acropolis, a pinnacle of human endeavour was attained, a moment of classic perfection which could neither be sustained nor repeated. At the same time, Angkor Wat may be seen as the logical culmination of a very long and continuous development in Khmer architecture: from the early, isolated tower shrines, to the 'god-mountain' – first natural, then artificial – crowned initially by one tower and later proliferating into the characteristic quincunx. The subsidiary features of the mythical Mount Meru, too, became progressively more complex. The axial stairs were defined by magnificent architectural and sculptural features, the turrets on the terraces expanded to continuous galleries, lavishly decorated and accented with central gateways and angle pavilions and the complete main shrine became but the centre-piece of a far larger composition of water-garden, architecture and sculptural elements, affording a sequence of visual impressions as varied, complex and carefully calculated in their spatial inter-relationships as those of any monument of the High-Baroque.

The approach to Angkor Wat is dramatic in the extreme. The deep shade of encircling jungle opens on to a spacious expanse of water, shimmering in the sunlight, the great moat, some 600 ft. wide, enclosing a rectangle nearly a mile square. A single monumental causeway lined by a magnificent balustrade of hooded serpents and lions spans the moat, like an umbilical cord, affording access to the triple entrance gateways, the two wider side-entrances being intended for elephants. The gateways are surmounted by unique, high, conical towers, reminiscent of the Papal Tiara, and are flanked by wide-spreading, arcaded galleries, forming a composition no less than eight hundred feet in width (Fig. 13).

Itself a stupendous work of architecture, the propylaeum provides a fitting prelude to the breathtaking vista that expands before one's gaze on emerging from its dark, deliberately constricted, chambers (Plate 73).

A thousand-foot long, raised, processional way, flanked midway by elegant library pavilions (Plate 91) and later by immense reflecting pools – microcosms of the Cosmic Oceans – leads to a cruciform podium from which the sovereign could watch processions and the performances of the temple dancers; and up to the main structure. Here is the apotheosis of the abode of the *Devaraja*, a temple-mountain of stupendous proportions flaring skyward in a vision of otherworldly splendour. Each of the terraces of the three-tiered pyramid has continuous galleries accented with gateways and towers, and elaborate stairways, and the plan is further enriched

88 Cham warriors with characteristic 'magnolia' head-dress; detail of a frieze depicting the great naval victory over the invading Cham forces; the Bayon, Angkor, Cambodia

89 Gable detail, Temple of Banteay Srei, Angkor, Cambodia

90 Causeway and south-gateway of Angkor Thom, Cambodia

91 Monks passing a 'library' on the causeway of Angkor Wat, Cambodia

92 Colossal head of a god from the balustrade of the causeway leading to a gate of Angkor Thom, Cambodia

by additional 'libraries' and subsidiary cruciform galleries. As one progresses towards the core of the structure, the emphasis changes subtly from the horizontal to the vertical. The gentle gradient of the lower flights of stairs becomes progressively steeper, symbolizing the inaccessibility of the central sanctuary (Plate 75), and the peaked-gables and towers coax the eye upward towards the culminating feature: five towers originally plated with gold and of the same, unique, tiara or lotus-bud form heralded by the propylaeum. They preside triumphant over monument and landscape, the central tower soaring to a height of over two hundred feet.

The miracle of Angkor Wat lies, above all, in the *ensemble;* in the fact that these numerous and complex elements have not merely been combined in an assemblage but have been orchestrated into a stupendous symphony in stone; that a Euclidean clarity of form in the total layout can be intuitively sensed by the spectator even if it can only be confirmed from the vantage point of the gods – or modern man: the air.

The sculptural decoration of Angkor Wat is, if anything, even more astonishing than the architecture. That the main temple alone should constitute the largest religious building in all history, covering an area as great as that of the largest pyramids, is astounding enough; that every square inch of such a structure should be carved and decorated, passes imagination. Yet so it has been, and with a loving care and skill which have infused the cold stone with pulsating life.

One stands dumbfounded at the mere thought of the labour involved in the six miles of exquisitely carved mouldings on the steps which line the great moat; or at the ten thousand stone pinnacles of lace-like intricacy assembled to crown each of the five towers; or at the two thousand life-size reliefs of *apsarases*, ranged like some celestial *corps de ballet* (Plates 77, 82 and 83), clothed in the most gorgeous stuffs and sporting unbelievable head-dresses, no two alike; or at the acres of background ornament, carved to represent the floral patterns found on Chinese silks; or, most of all, at the great bas-relief lining the lower cloistered gallery. One of the supreme masterpieces of world sculpture in terms of quality alone, this bas-relief is some six feet high and *over a mile* in length (Fig. 14).

The outer wall of the vaulted gallery is supported on piers and the large openings thus created, bathe the inner wall with its continuous reliefs in a flat, diffused light. Since the angle of illumination is not oblique, any deep undercutting of the stone would have added little to the effectiveness. This was realized by the artists of Angkor Wat who limited themselves to very low relief – the effect being almost that of a crisp, line drawing. The themes of the continuous reliefs are taken from Hindu mythology. Particularly noteworthy are the battle scenes from the *Mahabharata* and the *Ramayana*. The latter has already been mentioned in passing in connection with Ceylon, the setting for one of its main episodes: the abduction of Sita, wife of Rama, by the demon-king of Ceylon, the subsequent invasion of Lanka and the defeat of the demon-king with the help of Hanuman. At Angkor Wat the great battle between the forces of the demon-king and the cohorts of the monkey-general is depicted with enormous verve in a monumental composition. Never has a mêlée of struggling figures been depicted more convincingly or with greater artistic effect (Figs. 14 and 15). Providing an effective foil are such quiet compositions as the platoon of monkey-warriors sitting 'at ease' or the *pastorale* of Khmer herdsmen with their hump-backed, Zebu cattle shown in Fig. 17. The reason for the choice of this epic is that Rama was an incarnation of Vishnu (of whom the *Devaraja* was another manifestation). A relief some two hundred feet in length depicts scenes from the after-life in superimposed registers: heaven above and hell below. As invariably

93 A dwarf; relief from the inner corridor of the 'Elephant Terrace', Angkor Thom, Cambodia

94 Detail of typical towers with their colossal faces of the Devaraja-Bodhisattva guarding the cardinal points; The Bayon, Angkor Thom, Cambodia

95 Overall view of the Bayon, Angkor Thom, Cambodia

93

94

95

96

97

happens in such cases, the hell scenes are infinitely more intriguing. Here is the full complement of 'Thirty-Two Hells' to which defaulting vassals convicted themselves in the royal oath of allegiance. The miserable sinners condemned by Yama, Lord of the Underworld, are clubbed by huge demons as they are herded forward by ropes piercing their nostrils or cheeks to their appropriate punishment. Successive scenes show them gored by wild animals, grilled alive, boiled in giant kettles (for embezzlement or theft from holy-men or the sovereign) and devoured by worms. All the scenes, though portrayed with lurid relish, are at the same time enacted with balletic grace.

The scenes from the after-life share a wall with a rare secular scene: a royal procession, including a march-past of the army with some particularly vivacious figures of cavalry officers (Plate 80). The incredible patina of the stone is due to the habit among simple worshippers of pasting small pieces of gold leaf to the 'good characters' and stroking the surface of the stone in passing, thus imparting the lustrous gloss over a period of many years.

The hell scenes are the most naturalistic. The most monumental relief and possibly the most magnificent, is that depicting 'The Churning of the Sea of Milk'. The Gods and Titans (*asuras*) though in eternal conflict, formed a temporary alliance to procure the drink of immortality, *amrita*, or ambrosia. The body of the Cosmic Serpent, Vasuki, an avatar of Vishnu, was twined around the 'World-Mountain' placed in the primal void of the 'Sea of Milk' and teams of ninety-two demons and eighty-eight gods ranged on either side, grasped the head and tail of the serpent and enacted a celestial tug-of-war under the direction of Vishnu (Plate 81). They pulled the serpent back and forth and the mountain, pivoted on the back of the Cosmic Tortoise, Kurma – yet another manifestation of Vishnu – rotated, acting as a churning stick. As the Milky Ocean turned to butter, various symbols of power and delight emerged: *apsarases*, jewels, a milk-white charger and elephant, and Ghanvantari, the physician of the gods, bearing a bowl brimming with *amrita*.

Executed as it was, on a scale of imperial magnificence, the building of such a structure as Angkor Wat presupposed 'a high degree of economic and social integration, plus a government strong enough to command the labour and talents of vast numbers of trained participants. It reflected also the presence of an abundant food supply, a prosperous commerce, and a widely shared sensitivity to aesthetic values' (74) . . . the stone would appear to have been transported from the quarry to the site by means of a specially constructed canal, and was then 'cut into units of usable size and roughly dressed by thousands of stonecutters before being turned over to the skilled masons and sculptors entrusted with its final preparation. Behind the stonecutters were the construction foremen, the master architects and draftsmen. Still further removed were the Hindu scholars fully acquainted with the Sanskrit sources from which the Vishnu legend was drawn' (75). All told, we are dealing with a concurrence of favourable circumstances on a vast scale such as has occurred only a dozen times in world history.

Throughout the centuries of their greatness, the Khmers were in constant rivalry with the Chams, another Hinduized race of Malayo-Polynesian origin living in lower Annam. At its zenith, the Cham state extended from present-day Hue, southwards to the northern fringe of the Mekong delta. There were many cultural parallels between Champa and Cambodia, but their economies differed widely. Restricted by the narrow Annamese littoral which imposed a limit on food production and in turn on the population she could sustain, Champa turned to the

96 Naga or serpent balustrade from the landing-stage of the Sras-Srang or Royal Bath, Angkor, Cambodia

97 The overgrown Temple of Ta Prohm affords a good idea of the appearance of all Angkor when discovered a century ago. Angkor, Cambodia

98 Woman fanning her cooking-pot, detail of contemporary life on a relief at the Bayon, Angkor, Cambodia

sea. She developed an efficient fleet, commanded by a royal prince and often numbering as many as one hundred fortified vessels, which preyed on merchant shipping, exacting heavy tolls and at times descending to outright piracy. Relations between Champa and Cambodia became increasingly strained. The reign of Rajendravarman (944-968) saw the first of many wars between the two neighbours, and Suryavarman II conducted several inconclusive campaigns against Champa.

The successor of Suryavarman II was a cousin, Dharanindravarman II whose

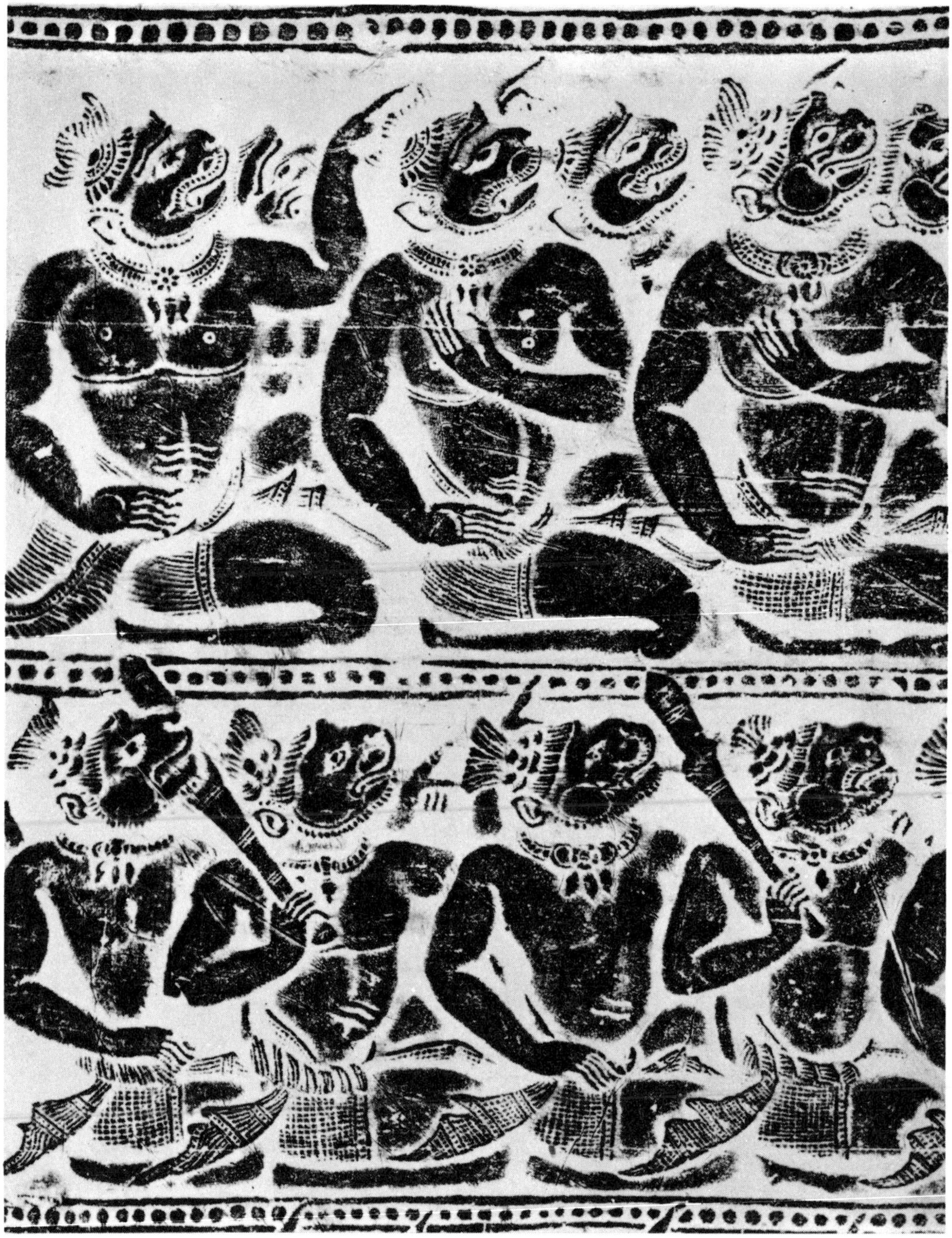

Fig. 15 Warriors of the monkey-general, Hanuman; detail from the great gallery of bas-reliefs at Angkor Wat. Original rubbing in the author's collection

short reign of a decade was marked by violent internal disturbances. On his death, his son and heir, later to be celebrated as Jayavarman VII, did not succeed directly. A relative, possibly a brother, became king as Yasovarman II. Various explanations have been proposed: that Jayavarman was away, possibly conducting a campaign in Champa, at the time of his father's death, and that Yasovarman took advantage of his absence to seize the throne; that Jayavarman, a devout Buddhist like his father, had voluntarily renounced his right to the throne to pursue the contemplative life; or that on Yasovarman's accession, he retired rather than cause a civil war. All evidence points to Jayavarman being a loyal subject of the new king.

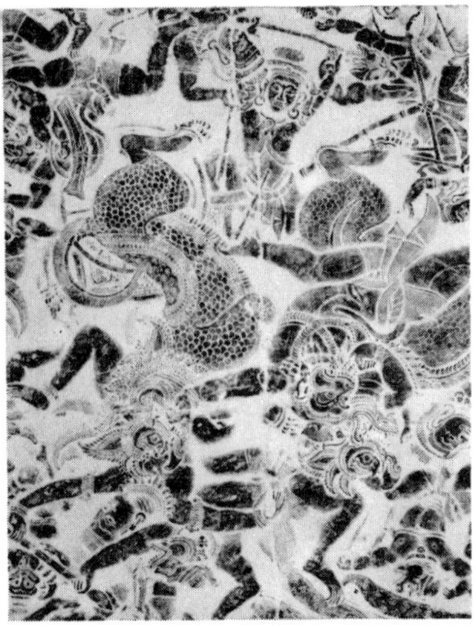

Fig. 16 Battle between the monkey-warriors of Hanuman and the followers of Ravana, the demon-king of Ceylon; detail from the *Ramayana* in the gallery of bas-reliefs, Angkor Wat. Original rubbing in the author's collection

After reigning a mere five years, Yasovarman II was deposed and killed by a minor Khmer chieftain, but once again Jayavarman, faced with a *fait accompli*, was seemingly content to remain in the background. At this juncture a bold and aggressive usurper seized the throne of Champa also and conceived a daring attack on Cambodia. Equipped and manned in the greatest secrecy, his fleet sailed down the sea-coast to the mouth of the Mekong and then up the river to the Great Lake of the Tonle Sap. His invasion took Angkor completely by surprise. The inadequate wooden stockage was stormed, the city pillaged and burnt, and the Khmer usurper executed. Convinced that the power of the Khmers had been dealt a deathblow, and themselves interested in loot rather than the administration of Angkor, the Chams soon departed from the ravaged capital, their ships weighed down almost to sinking with the rich spoils.

At long last, Jayavarman, by now a mature man of fifty, stepped forth from semi-retirement 'to save the earth from the sea of misfortunes into which it had been plunged', in the words of an inscription. He expelled the Cham invaders and quickly established his authority over dissident factions at home. By 1181 – only four years after the sack of Angkor – he had won a decisive naval victory over Champa and was able to celebrate his coronation as Jayavarman VII with great pomp at Angkor. His final act of revenge on Champa was planned with infinite patience and cunning. Only when potential allies of the Chams, such as the Annamite king of Dai-Viet in the north, had been won over with rich bribes, did Jayavarman VII strike. In 1190 the capital of Champa fell, and by 1199 proud Champa had been reduced to provincial status.

Under Jayavarman VII the Khmer Empire reached its ultimate expansion, extending from the lower Annamese coast on the east to the border of Pagan Burma on the west, and from Ventiane in present-day Laos far down the Malay Peninsula. His empire once secured, Jayavarman VII commenced a building programme of almost megalomaniacal proportions. He founded several new towns; erected innumerable Buddhist temples and charitable institutions, including more than a hundred hospitals, so distributed that there were facilities for the care of the sick in every region of the empire; and constructed a vast network of elevated military roads furnished with resthouses spaced at ten-mile intervals along their length. At Angkor itself he built more than his five predecessors combined, and if the classical perfection of the supreme moment in Khmer architecture, typified by Angkor Wat, eluded him, he left as his chief monument to posterity, if not one of the most beautiful, undoubtedly *the* most original building in the entire history of architecture: The Bayon.

The wooden palisades protecting Angkor had proved totally inadequate during the Cham attack, so Jayavarman surrounded his rebuilt capital, which he called Angkor Thom, or 'The Great Capital', with a stout stone wall eight miles in perimeter. The construction method employed was most ingenious: the earth excavated from the great moat, some hundred yards wide, was piled against the inner face of the wall, forming a raised boulevard or gallery. Small shrines were erected at the four corners and the rampart pierced by five gateways. The area of the square enclosed by the new walls was far smaller than that of the former Yasodharapura but, nevertheless, greater than that of any walled European city of mediaeval times, or even the Imperial Rome of Nero's day.

Two great avenues, on the north-south and east-west axes, divided the city into four quarters and there were great gateways where the avenues met and pierced the rampart. A fifth gateway afforded direct access from the east to the existing 'Grande Place' before the palace, now slightly displaced from the new east-west axis.

Two of Jayavarman's additions to the palace complex survive. The 'Terrace of the Leper King' is so-called from a much over-rated statue actually representing Yama, Judge of the Underworld. The terrace was most probably the scene of royal cremation rites. Far more magnificent is the adjoining 'Elephant Terrace' which served as the high podium of a series of audience or entertainment halls which, being of the customary light wood construction used for secular buildings, have long disappeared. The thousand-foot long façade facing the 'Grande Place' is decorated with a continuous monumental bas-relief of life-sized elephants (Plate 79). An inner corridor of the terrace contains some celebrated sculpture in very high relief, including the engaging figure of a dwarf (Plate 93).

Outside the city walls, Jayavarman built the Sras Srang, or Royal Bath, with its elaborate landing stages adorned with sculptures of lions and *naga*-balustrades (Plate 96).

The design of the five gateways of Angkor Thom provides a fitting prelude to the phantasmagoric vision of the Bayon. The high central entrance is flanked by sculptures of the sacred tricephalous elephant of Indra, its three trunks extended downward, foraging for lotuses. Above, the tower is carved with four gigantic faces, smiling enigmatically – likenesses of the God-King Jayavarman VII himself (Plate 54). The manner in which the mass and silhouette of the central tower is echoed by the pointed opening of the gateway below – a rather unfortunate, but strangely compelling positive-negative relationship – is fortuitous, being due to the destruction of the outer face of masonry with its original square-headed opening. But even this accident only contributes to the uncanny Surrealist effect, as if the most bizarre painting by Max Ernst had come to life.

The balustrades of the broad causeways that cross the moat at the gateways are formed by teams of stone colossi, gods on the one side and demons on the other, using the body of a gigantic serpent as a rope in their tug-of-war – or, rather, in their churning operation, for we have here another illustration of the 'Churning of the Sea of Milk', so dear to the Khmer heart. Instead of Vishnu presiding over the ceremony as in the great bas-relief of Angkor Wat, we have the visage of the God-King on high. The symbolism of the composition is thus that the gods and demons – the former distinguished by their benevolent expression and almond-shaped eyes, the latter glaring wide-eyed and with drooping mouths (Plates 92 and 52) – churn the Sea of Milk, or waters of the moat, using the *naga* king as a churning rope wound around the four-faced gateway-tower which serves as the churning-stick. The auspicious product of this collaboration between all the supernatural forces is that elixir of good fortune and longevity, the *Devaraja* or here, more accurately, the *Buddharaja* in the guise of the Bodhisattva Avalokitesvara, whose beneficent, all-encompassing gaze ensures the prosperity of the four quarters of the realm.

At the precise centre of Angkor Thom, where the two main arteries converged,

Jayavarman raised his personal 'god-mountain', the Bayon. Here no fewer than fifty towers, each carved with the same four smiling faces, jostle skywards (76). Instead of the serene, classical harmony of Angkor Wat, we have an almost nightmarish sense of confusion which, however, only serves to heighten the emotional impact of the monument: a haunting, brooding sculpture of Gargantuan proportions rather than a work of architecture.

The confused plan of the Bayon is partly the result of numerous changes effected as the work progressed. Henri Parmentier, the French archaeologist who worked on its restoration, maintains that 'it was begun to extend flat on one level only, but an enclosure of cross-shaped, foliated galleries was conceived and raised higher to frame a long-shaped sanctuary; these galleries and their sixteen towers were hardly constructed when it was decided to complete the interior rectangle by prolonging them at a lower level, and at the same time the two systems of galleries were linked by sixteen halls, the laterite foundations of which can still be seen on the sandstone paving of the outside courtyard; these made the abnormal building of the libraries necessary. But then, the King considered that the sanctuary as planned was too small, and, in order to install the present enormous unit, he almost blocked the interior galleries with the tremendous terrace which carries it.' (77)

There were further changes when, following Jayavarman's death, there was a violent, if short-lived, Sivaite reaction. Many Buddhist images were destroyed or mutilated, others were denatured to incorporate them within the Sivaite iconography (78). The giant face-towers of Avalokitesvara were spared. No doubt they were interpreted as *mukha-lingams*, or 'face-lingams', a form of the phallus incorporating the face of Siva, common enough in votive images, but never employed on so monumental a scale.

It is significant that repeated visits to the Bayon tend only to reinforce its stupendous impact. With familiarity, even the overall composition, at first sight so hopelessly confused, assumes some sense of order. Although, undoubtedly, to be classed as a failure from a strictly architectonic point of view, this surrealist masterpiece is imbued with a spiritual force so compelling that it succeeds in imposing its own seal of unity.

In judging Indian architecture we must never lose sight of the fact that the *raison d'etre* of the temple is as the dwelling place of the god, represented by his image. If Angkor Wat may rightly be considered the perfect earthly abode of a deity personifying the forces of clarity, harmony and order, the irrational aspects of divinity in its wedding of mystical aspiration and the dark streams of the subconscious, have received their perfect expression in the enigmatical smile of the Bayon, at the same time unnerving and reassuring (Plate 102).

Whereas the design of Angkor Wat represented the culmination of a long and continuous stylistic development, the Bayon was so unique and unexpected a flowering of the Khmer genius that it was most difficult to date. For many years it was supposed by the experts to have been built by the founder of Angkor in the ninth century as the central monument of his city of Yasodharapura. The reason for this mistake was the comparative crudity in the execution of the detail; this was falsely attributed to a primitive, formative phase rather than to its true cause: the haste of a monarch over-impatient to see his numerous great projects completed.

There is in this respect, a most striking parallel between the monuments of Jayavarman VII and those of another great conqueror and builder, Rameses the Great of Egypt, whose numerous grandiloquent structures, too, bear witness to an undue haste and the appropriation of material, 'second-hand' from earlier monuments. Careless workmanship, particularly in the poor bonding of the stones, with numerous superimposed vertical, or near-vertical joints, has been a prime cause for the poor preservation of the monuments of the Bayon period (79). But, paradoxically, it is precisely to its semi-ruined state that the Bayon owes much of its romantic charm. This is enhanced yet further by the fascinating texture of the stone, the grey and occasionally red sandstone being streaked with black and dappled with a leprous-looking, grey-white lichen (Plates 99 and 102). This brings to mind one of the most fascinating legends of Angkor: that of the Leper King. When Henri Mouhot, the French naturalist-explorer stumbled upon the ruins of Angkor and questioned the natives on their origin, he invariably received one of three answers: 'They were the work of the King of the Angels'; 'They built themselves'; or, 'They were the work of the Leper King'. This retention of the legend of the Leper King in the Cambodian folk-memory is all the more remarkable at a time when the very existence of Angkor had been all but forgotten. A thirteenth-century Chinese visitor to Angkor remarked upon the numerous lepers, neither scorned nor isolated in any way. This was attributed to the fact that one of their former kings had been afflicted by the disease. A popular supposition is that the king referred to was none other than the great Jayavarman VII, who turned to Buddhism for solace. Perhaps significant in this connection is the fact that the cult of Bhaisajyaguru, the Buddha in his manifestation as the 'Cosmic Medicine Man' or 'Divine Healer' was particularly favoured during his reign.

Fig. 17 Pastoral scene from the *Ramayana*, Angkor Wat, in the gallery of bas-reliefs. Original rubbing in the author's collection

One of the most fascinating features of the Bayon is the great gallery of bas-reliefs where, for the first time, scenes from Khmer history and everyday life, rather than Hindu mythology, predominate. A large cycle of reliefs is devoted to Jayavarman's wars with Champa. Curiously enough, the combatants would be indistinguishable, were it not for the characteristic, inverted, magnolia-shaped helmets of the Chams. The naval engagements are particularly impressive. In one scene the great war-canoes of the invaders with their elaborately-carved, Garuda figureheads race forward to the attack, the spears of the warriors poised menacingly; in another, two ships have locked in combat and a crocodile in the teeming waters claims a man who has fallen overboard.

The king, seated in a pavilion and surrounded by his courtiers, watches as grooms lead forth animals from his private zoo, including a rhinoceros, a strange-looking bird which may represent a cassowary and, somewhat surprisingly, a hare.

In a forest setting, cooks prepare an elaborate feast. An army of assistants scurries back and forth bearing trays of containers on their heads, while others kindle the fires, and a whole boar is popped into an enormous pot.

The difference in style between these reliefs and those at Angkor Wat is astonishing. We have moved all the way from an hieratic, aristocratic art to a popular form, full of fresh and spontaneous touches and as easily comprehensible as a comic-strip. This 'humanistic' transformation in so short a time must undoubtedly be attributed, at least in part, to the influence of Buddhism and its compassionate champion.

There is a pronounced sensuality, though still never a trace of eroticism, in the sculpture of Jayavarman's reign. While the *apsarases* of Angkor Wat, for all their full-blown charms, still have an air of reserve, those of the Bayon dance with Dionysian abandon. Particularly noteworthy are the triads of *apsarases* carved in very low relief on the pillars, and quite beyond compare the small bronze *apsaras* with its exquisite patina now in the Boston Museum of Fine Arts (Plate 71).

We have seen that the Hindu legend of the 'Churning of the Sea of Milk' received its finest artistic expression at Angkor. Considering the Khmer obsession with serpent lore, it is hardly surprising that Buddhist themes with strong *naga* associations should have proved equally popular.

The legend of the Mucalinda Buddha relates that while the 'Enlightened One' was seated in meditation beneath a tree, the forces of evil whipped up a terrible storm – 'against the cycle of the seasons'. Then Mucalinda, the giant *naga* who dwelt among the roots of the tree, realizing the Buddha's danger, crept forth, coiled his body seven times around the 'Enlightened One' and spread out his hood protectively as an umbrella. After seven days the storm subsided. Mucalinda then relaxed his coils, assumed the form of a courteous youth and paid homage to the Buddha. There is a particularly interesting sculpture of the subject in the Musée Guimet (Plate 76). The Buddha, manifest in the form of the *Devaraja* – evident from the crown and jewels, never found on conventional Buddha images (80) – sits meditating upon a throne formed by the coils of Mucalinda whose seven-headed hood forms an aureole around the Buddha's head.

The Khmer school of portrait sculpture which evolved in response to the *Devaraja* cult, occupies an extremely high position in world art. It manifests a rare synthesis, rivalled only by Egyptian art of the 'Old Kingdom' period, of individual portrait characteristics and an abstract, hieratic symbol of power. Although some earlier portraits may be even finer in execution, none is more moving than the superb head presumed to represent the great Jayavarman himself, now in the National Museum at Phnom Penh (Plate 103). The meditative expression and subtle smile, seeming to reflect an inner light of the spirit, could hardly be more fitting for this great king who, in the words of the foundation stele of one of his hospitals 'suffered more from the grief of his subjects than from his own ills'.

There are some striking parallels between the positions occupied by Jayavarman VII and Parakrama the Great in their people's destiny. Both came to the throne during unsettled times, when the country was rent by internal dissension and in dire danger from the traditional enemy: the Chams and Tamils, respectively. Both through their military prowess, statesmanship and great personal qualities ensured the safety of the realm, extended their dominion further than ever before,

Fig. 18 Gateway balustrade of Angkor Thom as it appeared in the latter half of the nineteenth century, from *Voyage d'exploration en Indo-chine*, by Francis Garnier, 1873

and ushered in a period of great prosperity and high culture. Both were humane and tolerant rulers whose religious devotion found expression in numerous charitable works. Both were great builders. Both reigns appeared to offer promise of a glorious future, but proved to be, rather, the magnificent last-flowering – an Indian Summer as it were – of their civilizations, for both monarchs through their constant wars of aggrandisement and titanic building programmes, seem to have sapped their people's energy beyond recovery.

The fall of the Sinhalese was swift and dramatic: barely a decade after the great Parakrama's death, Polonnaruwa lay in ashes. But although only a shadow of her former glorious self, Sinhalese culture survived and through her historical epics, the *Mahavamsa* and the *Culavamsa*, preserved a sense of continuity with the past. The fall of the Khmers was gradual, but ultimately so complete, that when the ruins of Angkor were rediscovered, the modern Cambodians were incredulous that their ancestors could have wrought such wonders.

Soon after the death of Jayavarman VII, a combined force of Khmers and Chams was defeated by the Annamites of North-Vietnam and shortly afterwards, Cambodia withdrew her army of occupation, leaving the Chams to contend as best they might with their aggressive northern neighbour. Champa was never again to constitute a real threat to Cambodia. A new and growing peril had, however, appeared in the form of the Siamese or Thais. From their original home in South China, Thai tribes had for centuries been moving southwards and settling in the central Menam valley, where they set up their own petty states under Khmer suzerainty. The march-past of the army of the Khmers and their vassals in the great bas-relief at Angkor Wat includes a Thai contingent, the artist obviously taking a rather malicious delight in emphasizing their oddities of dress and contrasting their rather raggle-taggle disarray with the Prussian discipline of the Khmer regiments.

The Mongols who were responsible for the fall of Pagan, also contributed indirectly to the collapse of the Khmer Empire. It will be recalled that it was the Mongol conquest of the kingdom of Nanchao that precipitated Narathihapati's fatal defiance of Peking. The conquest of Nanchao also sent a flood of Thai refugees southward to swell the existing Thai settlements.

The first major step towards Thai independence was taken when a Thai chieftain married to a Khmer princess – probably a daughter of Jayavarman VII – overthrew the Khmer governor in a province of the Menam valley and founded the Kingdom of Sukhothai. One of his sons, Rama Khamheng, the national hero of the Thais, consolidated their power and extended his dominion over large areas.

Several hypotheses have been put forward to explain the enigma of the fall of the Khmer Empire: that Jayavarman VII so overtaxed the resources and drained the energy of the nation that it was unable to withstand the onslaught of the Thais; that some natural calamity – fire, flood or pestilence – initially disrupted the irrigation system, that the population then turned to the 'dry method' in the cultivation of rice and that this caused laterization of the sub-soil, a rare chemical action which rendered the land unfertile; finally that the gentle creed of Buddhism, which in its extremely pacifist, Theravada form became dominant after 1300, was responsible. This reformed sect, in its emphasis on renunciation and detachment from the affairs of an 'illusory' world, might so have undermined the authority of the God-King that he could no longer command the implicit allegiance and unremitting toil of the populace – so essential to maintain the complex irrigation

99 Lichen-flecked towers of the Bayon, Angkor, Thom, Cambodia

100 Detail from a bas-relief at the Bayon: Cham archers in a forest; Angkor Thom, Cambodia

101 Cock-fight from a bas-relief at the Bayon, Angkor Thom, Cambodia

100

101

10

network on which the life-blood of the Khmer Empire depended.

No doubt a concurrence of several of these factors was responsible. Perhaps the single most important, was the introduction of Hinayana Buddhism. The role it was to play bears a remarkable analogy to that of Christianity in the Roman Empire. Both religions, despite their high moral standards, undermined the whole framework of the existing society through their emphasis on the personal aspects of salvation and their rejection of the worship of the God-King or God-Caesar. However, to lay the blame squarely on the new religion is to ignore an already prevailing disenchantment with the State Cult. 'Neither Christianity nor Hinayanism could ever have proved destructive had not the jaded *ethos* of the civilizations concerned, and the now outworn official cults, proved unequal to making the necessary adjustments and continuing the evolution on the old basis' (81).

Jayavarman VII had made just such adjustments by adapting Mahayana Buddhism to accord with the *Devaraja* cult and a similar adjustment could quite conceivably have been effected for Hinayana Buddhism. That this was not achieved was, no doubt, due at least partly to a special characteristic of the new religion. All the earlier 'imported' cults – whether Sivaite, Vishnuite or Mahayana Buddhist – had been imposed from above by the 'Indianized' elite of the court circle who had made sure that they were presented in a form which strengthened rather than weakened, the existing social structure. Hinayana Buddhism, on the contrary, was brought directly to the people. Its appeal was precisely that it offered release to the oppressed masses from the burdens imposed by the state and the greedy gods (82).

The thirteenth century saw a steady decline in Khmer fortunes. Not only did the Thai continue to annex territory but they made devastating raids on the Cambodian countryside. At the capital no more great monuments arose, but otherwise life continued much as before. Paradoxically, this unhappy period saw, if anything, a renaissance in the intellectual life of Angkor. 'Sanskrit verse was still written. Wise men abounded there, and foreign savants came, drawn by the reputation of this kingdom of high culture. Nowhere was knowledge more in honour. Scholars occupied the first charges of the State. They were on terms of familiarity with kings. Their daughters were queens. They themselves were royal preceptors, grand judges, ministers. There was a "King of Professors".' (83)

With the rise of a new and even more aggressive Thai dynasty centred around Ayuthia, within striking distance of Angkor, her days were numbered. But even then, the final debacle was long deferred. Only in 1431 was Angkor sacked by the Thais, evacuated soon after, briefly reoccupied and finally abandoned.

The tropical jungle engulfed the ruins, and apart from reports by sixteenth-century Jesuit missionaries of great buildings buried in the heart of the Cambodian jungle, in particular a reference to a lost temple 'called Onco and once as famous among the gentile as St Peters of Rome', the very memory of Angkor faded into oblivion.

It was Henri Mouhot, the French naturalist explorer, who rediscovered Angkor in the mid-nineteenth century. He was overwhelmed by the magnificence of these ruins hidden in the jungle and immediately sensed their importance. Of Angkor Wat he wrote: 'One of these temples – a rival to that of Solomon, and erected by some ancient Michael Angelo – might take its place beside our most beautiful buildings . . . Grander than anything left to us by Greece or Rome . . . it makes the traveller forget all the fatigues of the journey, filling him with admiration and

102 The smile of Angkor, at once unnerving and reassuring; detail of a colossal face on a tower of the Bayon, Angkor Thom, Cambodia

103 Head of a statue presumed to be that of Jayavarman VII. *National Museum at Phnom Penh*

delight, such as would be experienced on finding a verdant oasis in the sandy desert. Suddenly, and as if by enchantment, he seems to be transported from barbarism to civilization, from profound darkness to light' (84). Mouhot lamented that 'the very name of this lost race, like those of its great men, rulers and artists, seems destined to remain forever hidden among the rubbish and dust'. He would, indeed, be astonished if he could return today, and survey the growth of our knowledge over the course of a century. The 'illegible' inscriptions have yielded their secret and enabled us to reconstruct the main events of Khmer history. Together with the stylistic analyses of art historians, they have made it possible to establish the chronological sequence of the remains.

As regards monumental architecture and sculpture, we could hardly be more fortunate. We have one of the greatest legacies in stone of all time – perhaps *the* greatest. The great gap in our knowledge pertains to everyday life at Angkor. The Khmers cremated their dead so we are denied the invaluable testimony of tombs, so often serving as a durable repository for the necessities and luxuries of this life. The inscriptions though invaluable, are official in tone and severely limited, in their scope, and the skins and parchment used for writing have in this damp climate, long succumbed to rot and mildew. The bas-reliefs of the Bayon afford tantalising glimpses of life at Angkor and make us long all the more for the report of an eye-witness.

By the most sheer good fortune, just such an account survives in the report of Chou Ta-kuan, an envoy from the court of Timur Khan at Peking (85). Perspicacious and witty, if at times almost intolerably condescending in his attitude towards non-Chinese and, therefore, *ipso facto* 'barbarian' customs, his report is also extremely accurate, being corroborated by descriptions of buildings still extant and by the evidence of the bas-reliefs.

Chou Ta-kuan spent almost a year at Angkor during 1296-1297, literally at the eleventh hour of its greatness. Although Khmer power was waning fast, his account gives scant indication of its imminent fall. The economy still flourished – attested to by the very presence of the Chinese commercial mission of which he formed part – and in the capital, affairs were still conducted with the pomp and ceremony befitting a great empire.

'When the king rides forth' he writes, 'soldiers march at the head of the procession, followed by the standards, banners and musicians. Next comes a column of three to five hundred palace-maidens, clad in robes of floral pattern, with flowers in their hair and bearing candles, lit even in broad daylight. These are followed by another troop of maidens carrying the royal plate of gold and silver and a whole series of ornaments and insignia. Next come Amazons armed with spears and shields forming the private palace guard . . . and goat- and horse-drawn carriages, all decorated with gold. Then, preceded by innumerable red parasols, visible from afar, come the ministers and the princes, all mounted on elephants, followed by the wives and concubines of the king, borne in palanquins and carriages, or mounted on horseback and elephants, their gold-spangled parasols assuredly numbering more than a hundred. Finally the sovereign. He stands erect on an elephant whose tusks are sheathed in gold, and holds the precious sword of state in his hand. He is escorted by more than twenty white parasols, spangled with gold (86). Numerous elephants mill around him and yet another troop of soldiers provides him protection.'

'Twice a day the sovereign holds an audience for the affairs of government . . .

After waiting some time, one hears music far away within the palace . . . Without, a fanfare on conch horns greets the sovereign and an instant later two palace-maidens raise the curtain with delicate fingers and the king, sword in hand, appears standing at the window of gold. Ministers and people join their hands together and bow their foreheads to the ground. Only when the noise of the conches ceases are they permitted to raise their heads . . .When the audience is over the king leaves, the two maidens let fall the curtain and all rise. From this,' observes Chou Ta-kuan, 'it can be seen that a kingdom of barbarians though this may be, they know full well the meaning of royalty.'

'Both men and women, including the king, wear their hair in a chignon and have the upper part of the body bare, wearing only a small piece of cloth around the loins . . . Both use perfumes of sandalwood, musk and other essences most liberally. The pattern and quality of the cloth varies according to the status of the person . . . Among the stuffs worn by the sovereign are some worth three to four ounces of gold . . . Although cloth is woven in the country itself, it is also imported from Siam, Champa and India, the latter being generally the most prized for its fine workmanship.

The king usually wears a crown of gold. Occasionally, however, he is adorned only with a garland of sweet-smelling flowers similar to jasmin, entwined in his chignon. Around his neck he wears about three pounds of large pearls and around his wrists and ankles, and on his fingers, bracelets and rings of gold set with cats'-eyes.

Even the king goes bare-footed . . . the soles of his feet and the palms of his hands being tinted with a red dye . . . Among his subjects, only the women dye their soles and palms red . . . the men would not dare!'

'The king has five wives, one for the principal chamber and one each for the four cardinal points. As for concubines and palace maidens, I have heard a figure of three to five thousand mentioned . . . When a family has a beautiful daughter, they never fail to send her to the palace.'

Chou Ta-kuan was most intrigued – if not a little shocked – by the emancipation of women in Khmer society. Among the wealthier classes they had the same education as men and occupied such important positions as counsellors, royal secretaries, professors and even judges. Other Chinese writers, too, comment on the intellectual prowess and skill in science of Khmer women. This is surprising in a society based so closely on Hindu precepts. We have here a case in point of the persistent survival of ancient Austro-Asiatic mores 'In this country' writes Chou Ta-kuan, 'it is the women who engage in commerce. Thus, if a Chinese on arriving here straightway takes a wife, one of the chief reasons is to profit from her commercial aptitude. Each day a market is held from six to noon. They spread out a type of matting on the ground, each in the allotted place, for which, it is said, they pay a fee to the authorities . . .' The barter system generally prevailed in the market place, silver or gold being used only for large transactions. In this regard it is curious that the Khmers never developed a currency of their own. Among Cambodia's more exotic exports to China listed by Chou Ta-kuan were gutta-percha, rhinoceros horn (used as an aphrodisiac) and kingfisher feathers, employed to decorate the traditional bridal head-dress.

'Everyone says that Khmer women are extremely lascivious. A day or two after they have given birth, they sleep with their husbands. If a husband does not respond to their desire, he is abandoned. Again, if he is called away on some business, all goes well for a couple of nights, but very soon they are sure to say "I am not a spirit. How can I sleep alone?" '

The puberty rites of girls were particularly elaborate. Chou Ta-kuan gives a fascinating account of the customary deflowering ceremony. 'Between the age of seven and nine, in the case of girls from wealthy homes, and by eleven at the latest in the case of the very poor, a Buddhist or Taoist priest is appointed to deflower the young maidens . . . Each year the authorities choose a day of the month corresponding to the fourth moon of the Chinese . . . and proclaim it throughout the land. Every family where a girl is to undergo the ceremony informs the authorities and is given a wax taper on which a mark has been made. On the appointed day the taper is lit at night-fall and when it has burnt as far as the mark, the moment of defloration has arrived. A month before the chosen date . . . the parents choose a Buddhist or Taoist priest, according to their place of residence, each temple usually having its own clientele. The bonzes of repute are bespoken by the rich and noble families; the poor have little choice. Wealthy families give the priest gifts of wine, rice, cloth, silk-goods, *arec* and silver objects to the value of a hundred *piculs* . . . or at the very minimum ten.

If daughters of the poor chance to be already eleven without undergoing the ceremony, it is only because of the cost of the customary gifts . . . Certain people donate money for poor girls and this is considered a most worthy deed. Each priest may approach only one girl a year, and once he had made an agreement with one family, he is not allowed to enter into a contract with another.

On the chosen night a great banquet is given . . . and the parents seek out the priest with palanquins, parasols and music. Two pavilions are constructed of vari-coloured silk. In one the young girl is seated, in the other the priest. So deafening is the music that it is impossible to hear a word that is said. When the chosen moment has arrived, the priest enters the pavilion of the virgin, deflowers her with his hand and collects the first-fruits in some wine. It is averred that the parents, relatives and neighbours mark their foreheads with it, and even that they taste it. Some claim that the priest actually unites with the young girl but others deny this. Since Chinese are, however, not permitted to witness the event, it was impossible for me to determine the precise truth in this regard.'

'The women here age very quickly, due no doubt to marriage and child-bearing at too early an age. At twenty or thirty they resemble Chinese women of forty or fifty.'

'The country is frightfully hot and one cannot spend a single day – or night – without taking several baths. There are no bath-houses, but each family, or group of families, have their own pool. Both sexes enter the pool naked at the same time . . . The only restriction is based on age: the older members of the family do not bathe with the young . . .

Often, small groups of women go off together to bathe in the great river outside the town . . . They take off their clothes on the river bank . . . Sometimes there are thousands of them in the water, including women of the noble families, who incur no disgrace whatever, even though everyone can see them naked from head to foot. The Chinese, in their leisure hours, often have fun going to see this. I have even heard it said that there are those who enter the water to take advantage of the occasion.'

It was from Chou Ta-kuan that we quoted the legend of the 'Leper King'. The prevalence of the disease was generally attributed to the climate but Chou Ta-kuan had his own theory: 'In my humble opinion one catches this disease if one takes a bath immediately after sexual intercourse – the general practice among these people.'

Chou Ta-kuan stressed the gulf which separated the life of the privileged classes from that of the masses and cited many examples of the rigid stratification of society and the numerous sumptuary laws. Whereas the palace was roofed with lead and yellow-glazed tiles, and the homes of the nobles with clay tiles, those of the common people were simply thatched. Dimensions and design depended not only on wealth but on status. Thus, ordinary people would never have dared to put a single tile on their roofs. Their homes had neither tables, benches, basins nor pails. A clay pot was used for cooking rice and a frying pan to prepare the sauce. Halved coconut-shells served as ladles and leaves were fashioned into cups so expertly that even when full of liquid not a drop leaked out – all in sharp contrast to the homes of the nobles with their elaborate utensils of silver and even of gold.

Much of the menial labour was performed by slaves, members of a half-savage race called the Chuangs brought from the mountain regions (87). Many people had up to a hundred slaves; ten or twenty was considered a small number, while only the very poorest had none at all. Strong, young slaves were worth a hundred pieces of cloth, old and weak slaves could be bought for twenty or thirty pieces. Slaves appear to have had no rights whatever. They were not allowed to leave their master's house, slept outdoors between the pillars underneath the house and endured bodily punishment stoically without so much as flinching. If caught trying to escape, they were branded on the face and forced to wear an iron collar. So despised were they, that to call a Cambodian a 'Chuang' was the worst possible insult. In fact, even sexual intercourse with a slave was considered unthinkably degrading and never practised.

Chou Ta-kuan comments on the presence of the 'yellow-robed' monks of Theravada Buddhism at Angkor. A single remark betrays the impending danger. 'In the recent wars with the Siamese' he notes 'the countryside was completely devastated.'

Throughout, a conscious effort has been made to preserve the monuments without destroying the poetry of their jungle setting. Particularly inspired was the idea of leaving several temples, notably Ta Prohm (Plates 86 and 97), in the grip of the devouring vegetation – relaxed only sufficiently to ensure their accessibility and prevent further destruction – thus affording a vivid picture of the state in which all Angkor was found. Agile monkeys still cavort in the swaying tree-tops high above, while the light filters down through veils of foliage to ruins bathed in a silent, subaqueous penumbra; silk-cotton trees still sprout from the roofs of shrines and banyans send their gigantic, blanched roots groping like tentacles among the moss and lichen-flecked stones; orchids still brush the sensuous cheeks of sculptured *apsarases* and lianas entwine the colossal features of *Bodhisattvas* brooding over the ruins with the enigmatic smile of Angkor.

Notes

1 Once the Master addressed the disciples in the Deer Park at Benares:
'There are two ends not to be served by a wanderer. What are those two? The pursuit of desires and of pleasure which springs from desires, which is base, common, leading to rebirth, ignoble and unprofitable; and the pursuit of pain and hardship, which is grievous, ignoble and unprofitable. The Middle Way . . .avoids both these ends; it is enlightened, it brings clear vision, it makes for wisdom, and leads to peace, insight, full wisdom and Nirvana. What is this Middle Way? . . . It is the Noble Eightfold Path – Right Views, Right Resolve, Right Speech, Right Conduct, Right Livelihood, Right Effort, Right Recollection and Right Meditation. This is the Middle Way . . .

'And this is the Noble Truth of Sorrow. Birth is sorrow, age is sorrow, disease is sorrow, death is sorrow, contact with the unpleasant is sorrow, separation from the pleasant is sorrow, every wish unfulfilled is sorrow – in short all the five components of individuality are sorrow.

'And this is the Noble Truth of the Arising of Sorrow. (It arises from) thirst which leads to rebirth, which brings delight and passion, and seeks pleasure now here, now there – the thirst for sensual pleasure, the thirst for continued life, the thirst for power.

'And this is the Noble Truth of the Stopping of Sorrow. It is the complete stopping of that thirst, so that no passion remains, leaving it, being emancipated from it, being released from it, giving no place to it.

'And this is the Noble Truth of the Way which Leads to the Stopping of Sorrow. It is the Noble Eightfold Path – Right Views, Right Resolve, Right Speech, Right Conduct, Right Livelihood, Right Effort, Right Recollection and Right Meditation.'

Abridged form of the *Dhammacakkapavattana Sutta* or 'Sermon of the Turning of the Wheel of the Law' quoted by A. L. Basham in *The Wonder that was India*. London, 1954.

2 Many adherents of the Hinayana resent the implied limitation of the term and prefer instead the name *Theravada* (Doctrine of the Elders or of the Senior Order of Monks).

3 To the world at large India gave 'rice, cotton, the sugar cane, many spices, the domestic fowl, the game of chess and, most important of all, the decimal system of numeral notation.' A. L. Basham: *The Wonder that was India*. London, 1954.

He mentions, but discounts the Arab claim to have invented the decimal system. Significant, perhaps, is the Arab word for mathematics: *hindisat* (The Indian Art).

4 Ananda Coomaraswamy: *History of Indian and Indonesian Art*. New York, 1927.

5 *The Travels of the Chinese Monk, Fa-Hsien* (Fa-Hien). Translated by James Legge. First edition, Oxford 1886.

6 Pliny: *Naturalis Historia*.

7 The division, though generally indicative of the island's fortunes, is arbitrary. There was no dynastic break. The first king of the 'Lesser Dynasty' was, in fact, the son of the last of the 'Greater Dynasty'. The *Mahavamsa* was discovered by George Turnour, a most cultured and dedicated member of the British Civil Service in Ceylon. His translation of part of the *Mahavamsa* first appeared in print in 1836. The standard translation of both chronicles is that of Wilhelm Geiger (1912), recently re-published with critical addenda by the Government of Ceylon: *Mahavamsa* 1950; *Culavamsa* 1953.

8 The landing-place called Tambapanni, has recently been positively identified as being north of Puttalam on the west coast.

9 The year 543 B.C., according to the Sinhalese chronicles. Wilhelm Geiger in the introduction to his translation of the *Mahavamsa*, presents a convincing argument for 483 B.C., the date now more generally accepted for Gautama Buddha's death. Since Sinhalese chronology is reckoned from this event, and most authorities still adhere to the traditional date, we have done likewise to avoid confusion.

10 Although Buddhism did not acknowledge the rigid divisions of society inherent in the Hindu Caste System, there was firm belief that only members of the higher castes were fit to rule. Hence Vijayo's claim to *Kshatriya* (Warrior or Princely caste) ancestry, and the necessity to take a consort of *Kshatriya* birth.

11 H. Parker: *Ancient Ceylon*. London 1909.

12 (Ibid) We can be sure that Parker's researches in this case were, if anything, even more thorough than usual, for he had a personal interest in the Basawak-kulam. His first assignment on his arrival in Ceylon in 1873 as an irrigation engineer, was a survey of this reservoir, at that time rendered virtually useless by a large breach in the embankment. Its restoration was undertaken immediately afterwards, and it remains in working order today.

13 Recorded in the *Rajataringini* Chronicle and quoted by Sir James Emerson Tennent in *Ceylon*, London 1860.

14 Literally, a 'Queen-enclosure'; probably a corruption of *bisikotuva*, 'the enclosure where (the water level) drops'.

15 The word *vihara* refers specifically to a monastery but is also loosely used to cover 'image-house' and 'temple'.

16 *The Travels of the Chinese Monk, Fa-Hsien.* Translated by James Legge. First edition, Oxford 1886.

17 The *Dagoba*, or *Dagaba*, from the Sanskrit *dhatu* (a relic) and *garbha* (a womb, receptacle or shrine) is, strictly-speaking, applicable only to the portion of the *stupa* containing the relic chamber.

In Ceylon it is, however, commonly used to denote the entire structure.

18 The practice of allowing an elephant – usually a sacred 'while elephant' – to choose the site of a proposed monument was common in Ceylon and South-East Asia. We shall meet another celebrated case in the building of the Shwezigon Pagoda at Pagan.

19 Major Jonathan Forbes: *Eleven Years in Ceylon.* London 1841.

20 General de Beylié in *L'Architecture Hindoue en Extreme-Orient* 1904, contends that the columns of the Thuparama supported 'un toit à l'indienne, à étages superposés'.

21 This would seem to derive from a very ancient practice. In the *Mahavamsa* we read that King Devanampiya-Tissa visited the Bo-tree which was 'decked with manifold ornaments, gleamed with various jewels and garlanded with many-coloured flags'.

On the seemingly universal practice of decorating sacred trees with strips of stuff, see Richard Andree: *Ethnographische Parallelen und Vergleiche.* Stuttgart 1878.

22 It was common practice to transplant shoots of the historic Bo-tree to important Buddhist sites. Two particularly celebrated examples were that planted at Sravasti by Ananda and at Peshawar by Kaniska. The Bo-tree at Anuradhapura is the only survivor.

23 The Zebu bull is sacred to Siva, the god of creation, while the cow is regarded with particular reverence as a synonym for the all-nourishing mother-earth (*bhu-devi*).

24 The Pandyan kingdom with its capital most often at Madura, occupied the extreme south of the sub-continent.

The Cholyan kingdom to the north extended as far as Mysore and had several capitals, at Uraiyur in the suburbs of present-day Tiruchirapalli (Trichinopoly), Tanjore and later at Conjeeveram (Kanchipuram).

25 There are several alternatives in spelling this name. 'Dutthagamini' is generally used by Western scholars, while the 'Sinhalized' version 'Dutugemunu' is favoured by the present Nationalist regime.

26 The *Tirunansis* were the highest-ranking ecclesiastics in the Buddhist hierarchy.

27 The *Mahavamsa.* Unless otherwise stated, the source of historical quotations is the *Mahavamsa* and, for the 'Lesser Dynasty', the *Culavamsa.*

28 The standard form of ritual circumambulation, moving clockwise, in the same direction as the sun.

29 The ancient chronicles, anxious to give the maximum credit to their hero-king, imply that only the pinnacle, the enamelling of the dome with *chunam* (a highly-polished and extremely durable plaster finish), and some decorative adjuncts are attributable to the reign of his successor. Parker, however, visiting the stupa at Christmas 1886, shortly after a small portion of brickwork had slipped from the southern side of the dome, observed that this had exposed the finished but unplastered surface of an inner dagoba around which a shell of brickwork some twenty feet thick had been added. It would appear, therefore, that King Saddha Tissa first enlarged the whole structure and only then added the finishing coat of *chunam.*

30 Also known as the Miriswetiya or Maricavatti.

31 Sir James Emerson Tennent. *Ceylon.* London 1860.

32 An even larger one was commenced by Parakrama Bahu the Great at Polonnaruwa in the twelfth century, but never completed.

33 The visitor to Anuradhapura should be aware of the fact that the dagoba popularly known as the Abhayagiri (east of the Ruanweli) is actually the Jetavana; and that that known as the Jetavana (north of the Ruanweli) is the Abhayagiri Dagoba of the ancient chronicles. The two names seem to have been accidentally interchanged many years ago.

34 This appointment of the sister's son as commander-in-chief seems to have been traditional in ancient Ceylon. The relationship between the king and nephew – by a sister only – is always described as that between father and son. We have here, no doubt, a survival from an earlier matriarchal line of succession in India and Ceylon.

35 Renditions by W. G. Archer of the translations by S. Paranavitana, quoted in *Ceylon, Paintings from Temple, Shrine and Rock.* New York Graphic Society for Unesco, 1957.

36 (Ibid)

37 (Ibid)

38 Polonnaruwa, alias Pulatthipura, Pulastipura, Kalingapura, or the modern Topawewa or Topawa, was on the site of the extremely ancient Wijitapura. It had been a place of royal residence since the time of King Aggabodhi III in the early seventh century.

39 Perhaps a reference to such twisted baroque columns as those we shall see at the *Nissanka-lata-mandapaya* or 'Floral Altar'.

40 The sacred Tooth of the Buddha is said to have been retrieved from his funeral pyre by the Sage Khema and was brought to Ceylon concealed in the hair of an Indian princess, fleeing from her beleaguered homeland. Fa-hsien left a graphic account of a 'Festival of the Tooth' at Anuradhapura in the fifth century A.D., which might well be a description of the annual *Perehera* procession at Kandy today, so little has the ceremony changed

during the course of a thousand five-hundred years. Although a late arrival in Ceylon, compared to the sacred collar-bone and alms-bowl, the tooth relic rapidly attained pre-eminent status. Enshrined in a jewel-studded casket, it resided in splendid state during periods of prosperity, and in times of danger was the first treasure to be carried to safety, for so closely had it become identified as the palladium of royal office that its possession, even by a usurper, lent his claim to sovereignty a measure of legality. The sacred relic underwent many vicissitudes, culminating in its capture and ceremonial destruction by the Portuguese in a characteristic display of religious intolerance. Although there is reason to believe that the original tooth may well have been a genuine relic of the Buddha, the present tooth would appear to be a substitute after the Portuguese *auto-da-fé*.

41 Indian bestiaries describe the *makara* as having the tail of a dolphin, the feet of a lion, the trunk of an elephant, the teeth of a crocodile, the eyes of a monkey and the ears of a pig.

42 Also known as the Buddha-sima-Prasada or the Jetavana Monastery.

43 The Pallava style as exemplified by these masterpieces of rock-cut architecture and sculpture, seems to have exerted a profound influence on Sinhalese art.

44 H. Parker: *Ancient Ceylon*. London 1909.

45 Robert Knox: *An Historical Relation of the Island Ceylon*. London 1681.

This unseemly behaviour may reflect an intended phallic symbolism in the uniting of the hooks of the goddess and husband – probably a play on the reproductive symbols of *lingam* and *yoni* – and this suspicion would seem to be confirmed by Pattini's identification in another manifestation with Durga, Consort of Siva, the Creator, whose symbol is the phallus.

The cult of Pattini Devi is a perfect example of the tangle of influences, animistic, Hindu and Buddhist, to be found in the religious life of Ceylon, at least at the popular level.

46 For a most interesting discussion of the symbolism of the lotus pedestal in Buddhist art see – Heinrich Zimmer: *The Art of Indian Asia: Its Mythology and Transformations*. New York 1955.

47 An interesting comparison is afforded by the representation of Avalokitesvara Padmapani in the celebrated thirteenth-century fresco in the Nandamannya Temple at Pagan in Burma (Plate 49).

48 The *bhikkhus* and *bhikkhunis*, the novices of both sexes, and the *samaneras* or young girls who were being prepared for the profession of nuns.

49 Also known as Hmawza and Old Prome.

50 cf: Reginald Le May: *The Culture of South-East Asia*. London.

51 John F. Cady: *South-East Asia: Its Historical Development*. New York.

52 Heinrich Zimmer: *The Art of Indian Asia: Its Mythology and Transformations*. New York 1955.

53 The *MAHA YAZA WIN TAW KYI* or *Glass Palace Chronicle of the Kings of Burma*, translated by Pe Maung Tin and G. H. Luce. Oxford 1923.

54 Literally: 'The Three Baskets' (*Pitakas*), from the fact that the long strips of prepared palm-leaf on which the texts were written were originally stored in baskets.

55 Known as *zedi* (derived from the Pali *cetiya*) in Burma. To avoid burdening the reader with yet another strange word, I shall stick to the more familiar *stupa*.

56 Alexander B. Griswold: *The Art of Burma*. New York 1964.

57 Hence the unlikely name *Erawan* (White Elephant) chosen for Bangkok's newest luxury hotel.

58 The Buddhist equivalent of *Hagia Sophia*.

59 Charles Duroiselle in the *Memoirs of the Archaeological Survey of India* (No. 56, 1937) also remarks on points of similarity to the Ananda in temples depicted on terra-cotta votive tablets found at the Pyu capital of Old Prome.

60 It is perhaps significant that such temples are known to the people as *gu* (from the Pali: *guha*, a cave).

61 Henry Yule: *Narrative of the Mission of the Governor-General of India to the Court of Ava*. London 1858.

62 Than Thun *Social Life in Burma A.D.* 1044-1287, Journal of the Burma Research Society XLI, quoted by John Cady in *South-East Asia: Its Historical Development*. New York.

63 After the battle the victorious Mongols used Burmese prisoners to recapture two hundred elephants which were incorporated into their army. Henceforth, Marco Polo informs us, an elephant battalion formed an integral part of every army of the Great Khan.

64 The Japanese alone in Asia managed to flaunt the Great Emperor successfully. Having subdued Korea, Kublai Khan sent emissaries to Japan demanding her submission. These were summarily put to death. But the action of the Kamakura Shoguns, though audacious in the extreme, was at least not patently suicidal. They had the backing of a powerful and extremely well-organized military machine and were separated from Kublai Khan's wrath by the ocean. The day was saved when the Emperor's great punitive Armada sustained critical losses from a providential typhoon, the *kamikaze* or 'Divine Wind', the name adopted by Japan's suicide pilots during the Second World War.

65 For example: Georges Coedès: *Les Etats Hindouisés d'Indochine et d'Indonésie*. Paris 1948.

66 The similar relationship between *Garuda*, the avian vehicle of Vishnu, and the *naga* in Hindu mythology does not necessarily posit an Indian origin, 'for the Austro-Asiatic civilization apparently penetrated in some unexplained fashion in pre-Aryan times to north India, a circumstance which may have

contributed a similarity of cultural traditions affording a basis for appropriation in historic times by the peoples of South-East Asia of many aspects of a mature Hindu civilization' – a resumé by John Cady in *South-East Asia: Its Historical Development.* New York, culled from the arguments propounded by D. G. Hall in *A History of South-East Asia.* London 1955.

67 Recorded by the tenth-century Arab historian, Abu Zaid Hasan.

68 Lawrence P. Briggs: *The Syncretism of Religions in South-East Asia*, Journal of the American Oriental Society LXXI (1951).

69 'Un réseau hydraulique' is the telling phrase used by Bernard Groslier who, with the aid of aerial photography, has made an extensive survey of Khmer agricultural hydraulics. His findings are summarized in *Angkor et le Cambodge au XVIe siècle d'après les sources portugaise et espagnoles.* Paris 1958.

70 After the deity, Harihara, a synthesis of Siva and Vishnu in one anthropomorphic manifestation. This cult of the union of opposites was at times extremely popular among the Khmers, chiefly during pre-Angkorean periods.

71 For a fascinating exposition of the many analogous features in the rise, glory and fall of the Khmer and Roman Empires see H. Quaritch Wales: *Angkor and Rome.* London 1965.

72 This observation does not apply to such pre-Angkorean works as the celebrated seventh-century Harihara from Prasat Andet or the Lokesvara (Avalokitesvara) of the Stoclet Collection in Brussels. In both, the carving is equally sensitive throughout.

73 Lawrence Briggs: *The Ancient Khmer Empire.* Philadelphia 1951.

74 J. F. Cady: *South-East Asia: Its Historical Development.* New York.

75 (Ibid)

76 The similarity of style between the gateways of Angkor Thom and the Bayon is not due solely to the fact that they date from one reign. They were conceived as one entity, the city wall doubling as the symbolic girdle-wall of the temple, the moat serving as the indispensable water-garden, 'so pleasing to the gods'.

77 Henri Parmentier: *Angkor.* Reprint, Saigon 1959.

78 For many years there was a bitter controversy among scholars as to whether the Bayon was a Buddhist shrine appropriated to Sivaite use or vice versa. We now have incontrovertible evidence that the former was the case. During restoration it was discovered that where a modification of the design during construction had hidden earlier completed work, the covered images displayed unmistakably Buddhist characteristics, while similar images, which had remained visible had been altered to conform to Sivaite iconography.

79 Unlike the builders of Pagan, the Khmers abided by the Indian prohibition of the true arch 'that never sleeps', using a system of corbelling to bridge openings. This not only severely limited the span but has been a prime cause of the ruin of many monuments.

80 When the Sage abandoned his life of princely ease, he divested himself of all finery. Only the distended lobes of his ears – a customary iconographic symbol – testified to the heavy earrings he had formerly worn and thus to his royal status.

81 H. Quaritch Wales: *Angkor and Rome: A Historical Comparison.* London 1965.

The most pertinent analogies in this most imaginative and fascinating book relate to the period of the 'Decline and Fall'.

82 Bernard Groslier in *The Arts and Civilization of Angkor*, New York, quotes a single temple as having a personnel of '18 High Priests, 2740 officiants, 2202 assistants and 615 dancing girls', and including in its treasury 'a service of gold plate weighing more than five tons and an almost equal weight of silver, 35 diamonds, 40,620 pearls, 4540 precious stones, 967 Chinese veils, 512 beds of silk, and 523 parasols . . . A single festival consumed more than 165,744 wax candles'. Needless to say, whole villages were dedicated to the upkeep of a single such shrine.

83 Louis Finot, quoted by George Maspero in *Un Empire Colonial Francais: L'Indochine.* Paris 1929.

84 Henri Mouhot: *Travels in the Central Parts of Indo-China.* London 1864.

85 Chou Ta-Kuan (Chou-Ta-Kouan): *Memoires sur les Coutumes du Cambodge*, translated by Paul Pelliot. Latest edition, Paris 1951.

86 The use of a white umbrella as the insignia of royal power is widespread in South-East Asia: Of Hindu origin, it symbolizes the protective *Dharma* or 'Firmament of the Law', which the ruler undertook to uphold at his coronation.

87 This is the only type of slave mentioned by Chou Ta-Kuan. Between the Chuangs and the freemen-commoners came a higher category of slave 'including debtors, war-prisoners, and descendants of leaders of rebellion. Official grants of foreign war-prisoner slaves to monasteries and temples were considered laudatory acts of piety' – John F. Cady: *South-East Asia: Its Historical Development.* New York.

Index